# ROCKS &
# MINERALS

Published in the United States and its territories and Canada by
HAMMOND WORLD ATLAS CORPORATION
Part of the Langenscheidt Publishing Group
36-36 33rd Street, Long Island City, NY 11106
EXECUTIVE EDITOR Nel Yomtov
EDITOR Kevin Somers

Produced for Hammond World Atlas Corporation by

MOSELEY ROAD INC.
129 MAIN STREET
IRVINGTON, NY 10533
WWW.MOSELEYROAD.COM

MOSELEY ROAD INC.
PUBLISHER  Sean Moore
ART DIRECTOR  Brian MacMullen
EDITORIAL DIRECTOR  Lisa Purcell

SENIOR EDITOR  Amber Rose
DESIGNERS  Terasa Bernard,  Joanne Flynn
CARTOGRAPHY  Neil Dvorak
EDITORIAL ASSISTANT  Rachael Lanicci

Printed and bound in Canada

ISBN-13: 978-0843-719321

# HAMMOND UNDERCOVER™

# ROCKS & MINERALS

## NANCY HAJESKI

**HAMMOND** World Atlas
Part of the Langenscheidt Publishing Group

# Contents

# Extraordinary Rocks and Minerals

**R**ocks and minerals are everywhere. In large cities, they lie underfoot in the streets and pavements and tower over your head as the skeletons of skyscrapers. In the suburbs, rocks and minerals adorn garden paths and stand as memorials in cemeteries. In the country, they're more obvious parts of the landscape—you've probably crossed a brook on stepping-stones or used rocks as handholds while climbing a steep hill. Rocks and minerals are even high overhead in the form of planets, moons, and stars. Rocks are found around the house—you may use them for sharpening tools or grinding spices. Minerals make up the coins jingling in your pocket and the white stuff—salt—that you sprinkle over your French fries.

Rocks are everywhere, from your local lakeshore to the farthest reaches of the universe.

With a rich variety of colors, polished rocks make beautiful displays.

## As Old as Time

Because rocks and minerals are everywhere around us, they may seem ordinary and commonplace, but you shouldn't take them for granted. Even the most humble paving stone, chunk of gravel, or grain of sand has a fascinating history, and it is quite likely millions of years old.

## A Closer Look

The next time you see a rock, pick it up and examine it closely. Ask yourself some key questions: What color is the rock? Is it dense and opaque, or does it have a glasslike surface that you can almost see through? Are its edges crisply sharp or softly rounded? Does it feel heavy for its size, or lighter than you'd expect? Does the rock look as if it is made up of just one material, with little variation in color or texture, or does it have small deposits of other substances? Think about where it may have come from—did a volcano thrust it up from the core of the earth, did it tumble from the side of a mountain, or did currents from the depths of the sea carry it to where you've picked it up? These are all questions scientists ask themselves when they want to identify a specific rock or mineral.

In the following pages, you, too, will learn how to identify rocks and minerals—the elemental building blocks of rocks. You will also discover how they originated and where they are found throughout the world, as well as how science, physics, industry, architecture, commerce, and space technology utilize them.

You may begin to look at rocks and minerals in different ways, not just as ordinary, everyday objects, but as relics of planet Earth's turbulent past and as key components of its future.

Next time you pick up a rock, think about its origins. This piece of pumice, for example, has a violent history. Millions of years ago, a volcano spewed superheated lava from its depths, which solidified into this highly porous rock.

# Identifying Minerals

Minerals are the building blocks of rocks, so it's important to know how to recognize them when you try to identify various rock samples. Identification can be tricky because some minerals have very similar chemical makeups, yet appear quite different to the naked eye. You can only conclusively identify minerals by X-ray—which determines their structure—and by chemical analysis—which determines their composition. Still, scientists can rely on several ways to identify minerals based on their physical properties alone, including the following.

## Color

Color is usually the first thing we notice about an object. The color in minerals, which are often more colorful than rocks, comes from light—the absorption or lack of absorption of various wavelengths (color is determined by the length of wave of light). When white light, which contains wavelengths of all colors of the spectrum (red, orange, yellow, green, blue, indigo, and violet), enters a mineral, it will absorb some colors, while emitting others. This is because certain elements have electrons that absorb and then emit different color wavelengths. The presence of these elements in a mineral, sometimes only in trace amounts, will give it a particular color. Some elements that produce specific colors are:

- **cobalt**—blue
- **copper**—blue-green
- **chromium**—orange-red

Rhodonite. The manganese in this mineral gives it its distinctive rose pink striping.

- **iron**—red
- **manganese**—pink
- **nickel**—green
- **uranium**—yellow
- **vanadium**—red-orange

Amber, which is fossilized tree sap, displays a resinous luster.

## Luster

Luster refers to the way a mineral's surface absorbs (takes in), reflects (bends), or refracts (distorts) light. The terms applied to luster include:

- **adamantine**—brilliant diamondlike or gemlike crystal
- **dull**—flat, nonreflective
- **fibrous**—strandy, textured
- **greasy**—oily
- **gumdrop**—the appearance of a hard candy
- **metallic**—gleaming, reflective
- **pearly**—lustrous
- **pitchy**—the look of tar
- **pesinous**—similar to dried glue or gum
- **silky**—finely textured
- **submetallic**—low luster, reflecting little light
- **vitreous**—glasslike
- **waxy**—dull, soft looking

Smoky quartz. Radiation can produce colors in minerals by damaging their crystalline structures. Smoky quartz is a result of exposure to radioactive minerals in the earth.

## Crystalline Structure

Each mineral has what is called a crystalline structure, reflecting the arrangement of the molecules in the mineral. Typically, different minerals that form crystals in the same pattern have a lot of characteristics in common.

## Cleavage

Cleavage describes how a mineral splits apart. It is a reliable identification tool because the same mineral will always display the same cleavage. Scientists usually rate a rock's cleavage as perfect, good, imperfect, or poor. There are three ways to judge if a mineral has good cleavage:

- The crystal should break smoothly along a parallel line, revealing a flat crystal face.
- This breakage should be reproducible, meaning it can be repeated over and over.
- The cleavage planes must match the crystal's symmetry.

## Fracture

Fracture occurs when minerals break along noncleavage planes. Fresh fractures allow you to see a mineral's true color. There are six basic types of fractures:

- Conchoidal is a smooth circular breakage, frequently seen in obsidian.
- Subconchoidal fracture is also smooth, but less rounded than conchoidal.
- Uneven fracture shows no symmetry.
- Jagged fracture has rough points. Metallic minerals, such as copper, typically show jagged fractures.
- Splintery fracture occurs in fibrous minerals.
- Earthy fracture resembles broken clay and tends to occur in loosely consolidated minerals.

The mineral copper shows jagged fracture, with rough points.

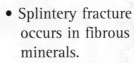

## ROCK CLEAVAGE

Cleavage in one direction example: muscovite

Cleavage in two directions example: feldspar

Cleavage in three directions example: halite

Cleavage in two directions example: calcite

A magnet will attract certain minerals, such as nickel, iron, cobalt, and magnetite.

### Magnetism

Only a few minerals display magnetism, which means that they will attract iron. Magnetism occurs when there is an imbalance in the arrangement of iron ions. Some magnetic minerals—magnetite and maghemite—are strong enough to lift a large nail. Others—chromite and franklinite—can barely move the pointer on a compass. To test for magnetism, hold a magnet on a string near the specimen and look for it to move toward the specimen.

Talc is so soft that you can scratch it with your fingernail. This mineral, which rates a 1 on the Mohs scale of mineral hardness, has a greasy luster.

### Streak

Minerals of one color often display a different color when they are rubbed on an unglazed white tile. This occurs when the powdered form of the mineral contains trace elements that show up in a streak but are not visible on the original specimen. Also, the surface color might not reflect the true chemical makeup of the mineral. Pyrite, or fool's gold, for example, turns black on a streak plate, but real gold is always yellow.

### Electrical Properties

Some minerals, such as sulfur or topaz, give off electrical charges when rubbed. Thin slices of quartz can actually control radio frequencies. If you heat tourmaline crystals, they give off opposite electrical charges at each end.

### Hardness

All rocks seem hard to the touch, but some are harder than others. Hardness, which rarely varies from specimen to specimen, depends on the strength of a mineral's chemical bonds. Scientists typically measure hardness in a laboratory. The Mohs hardness scale, developed by German mineralogist Friedrich Mohs in 1812, is based on one mineral's ability to scratch another, softer mineral. The Mohs scale rates the following minerals from softest to hardest:

1. talc
2. gypsum
3. calcite
4. fluorite
5. apatite
6. orthoclase
7. quartz
8. topaz
9. corundum
10. diamond

So, if an unknown mineral can scratch quartz, but is unable to scratch topaz, it falls between 7 and 8 in hardness. The Mohs scale does not rate degree of hardness from one mineral to another, so scientists have designed an absolute hardness scale that assigns a rating to each mineral. Soft talc earns a 1, apatite is a 48, corundum is a 400, and diamond, the hardest natural substance, rates a whopping 1,500.

### Specific Gravity

Specific gravity measures the density of a mineral by comparing it to the density of water, which is 1 gram per cubic centimeter. If a mineral is twice as dense as water, it receives an SG rating of 2. Most minerals in the earth's crust have an SG of 2.75.

### Fluorescence

A number of minerals are capable of emitting light. Fluorescent minerals contain chemicals that glow bright red, green, yellow, or blue when exposed to ultraviolet (UV, or black) light. Fluorite, benitotite, gypsum, sodalite, and hardystone are all fluorescent. If you remove the light source, and the mineral continues to glow, the result is called phosphorescence. When heating the specimen produces light, the mineral is called thermoluminescent. If the mineral emits light when you strike or crush it, it is considered triboluminescent.

## ROCK STARS
### Glowing with Pride

FRANKLIN, NEW JERSEY, calls itself the "Fluorescent Mineral Capital of the World." This area, in the northeast corner of the state, boasts deposits of willemite and calcite, both fluorescent minerals, as well as scores of other rare minerals. A recent count tallied 356 minerals, including 28 that are unique to the area. The Franklin Mineral Museum offers educational displays for students and a life-sized mine simulation. Visitors can "prospect" for specimens in the 15-acre (6 hectare) Buckwheat mineral dump—where new minerals are still discovered—and then check out the fluorescence of their finds under a black light inside the museum.

You can't judge a rock at first glance. A seemingly ordinary-looking grayish brown specimen, below, reveals its brilliant fluorescence under an ultraviolet light. At left, the mineral hydrozincite in the sample glows blue, calcite glows red, and willemite glows green.

# Revealing the Atom

Ever since ancient Greek and Indian philosophers theorized that the atom was the smallest unit of matter, scientists have been trying to unlock its secrets. Minerals have played key roles in that quest and in the creation of atomic energy. By studying radioactive minerals—ones containing elements that give off alpha-, beta-, and gamma-ray emissions—scientists in the twentieth century were finally able to probe the structure of the atom.

## Protons, Neutrons, and Isotopes

Why do these emissions occur in certain minerals? The number of protons in the nuclei of their atoms identifies elements. Oxygen atoms have 8 protons, for instance. In addition to protons, the nuclei contain uncharged particles called neutrons. Each element also has different isotopes, atoms in which the number of protons are always the same, (for example, 6 protons for carbon), but the number of neutrons varies. If the nucleus in an isotope is unstable, the isotope will be radioactive. This is especially true if the isotope's nucleus is very large, containing 83 or more protons, such as in uranium and plutonium. Scientists call the loss of energy from these unstable isotopes "radioactive decay," and the rate of decay is called a "half-life." By measuring their half-life, scientists calculate the age of ancient rocks.

Uranium ore, which is weakly radioactive. A uranium atom has 92 protons and between 141 and 146 neutrons in its nucleus.

## ROCK STARS
### "Madam, I'm Atom"

PHYSICIST AND CHEMIST MARIE CURIE was born Maria Skłodowska in Warsaw, Poland, in 1867. As a student in Poland and France, Curie became fascinated by the radioactive properties of certain minerals. After finishing school, she worked in Paris with her physicist husband, Pierre Curie, focusing on extracting uranium from a complex mineral called pitchblende. In 1898, the Curies discovered that pitchblende contained a substance even more radioactive than uranium. They called this new element polonium in honor of her homeland. That same year, the Curies also discovered the element radium, named for its intense radioactivity, a term they coined.

In 1903, Curie won the Nobel Prize in physics and, in 1911, another one for chemistry. Her discovery of radium provided scientists with a radioactive source that allowed them to study the structure of the atom and opened the door to the Atomic Age of the later twentieth century.

Pierre and Marie Curie. The Curies had no idea how dangerous radioactive elements are and often carried "hot" specimens in their pockets. Marie died from aplastic anemia, a weakening disease that resulted from exposure to large quantities of radiation.

### Dangerous Rays

Gamma rays are the most dangerous emissions. These high-energy photons can damage living cells, but thick layers of lead or concrete can shield you from gamma rays. Beta rays travel only a few feet (1m) before the air absorbs them, but can penetrate a layer of aluminum. Alpha rays travel 6 inches (15 cm) or less, and several sheets of paper can block them.

### Which Minerals Are Naturally Radioactive?

Any mineral containing potassium, uranium, or thorium is likely to be radioactive. But, because radioactivity exists in many natural substances—including human beings—it's not unusual for minerals to emit low levels of radiation.

## The Geiger Counter

THIS PORTABLE DEVICE, known as the Geiger counter, allows scientists to tell if a substance has radioactive properties. The handheld Geiger-Müller tube contains a negatively charged wire surrounded by gas. When exposed to radioactive material, the gas is partially ionized, and its molecules generate an electrical charge. This charge sends short bursts of current through the tube to the measuring unit. The measuring unit picks up the bursts and transmits them as clicks through headphones. The higher the level of radioactivity, the more frequent the clicks.

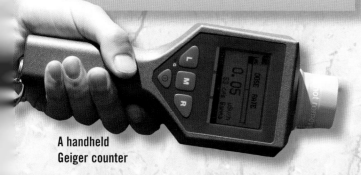

A handheld
Geiger counter

## WHERE ARE THEY?

Radioactive minerals are found worldwide.

- **autunite**—Autun, France; Portugal; Washington State; Zaire
- **bastnasite**—Greece; Balkans; Hungary; Mountain Pass, California; Ontario; Sweden
- **betafite**—Lake Baikel, Russia; Malagasy Republic
- **carnotite**—Arizona; New Mexico; Utah
- **cuprosklodowskite**—Congo
- **davidite**—south-central Australia; Bengal, India; Idaho; South Dakota
- **euxenite**—Colorado; Madagascar
- **fergusonite**—Norway; Texas; Virginia
- **gummite**—Australia; Central Europe; New Hampshire; Rocky Mountain states; United States East Coast; Vancouver, Canada
- **monazite**—south-central Australia; Madagascar; Malagasy Republic; North Carolina; Virginia
- **parsonsite**—France
- **samarskite**—Black Sea; Caspian Sea; southern Norway; Urals
- **schroeckingerite**—Utah, Wyoming
- **thorianite**—Madagascar
- **thorite**—Connecticut
- **thorium**—Australia; Brazil; India; Madagascar; Russia; Sri Lanka; United States
- **torbernite**—Australia; Cornwall, England; Czech Republic; North Carolina; Zaire
- **trinitite**—New Mexico
- **tyuyamunite**—southwest Africa; Central Europe; Colorado; Kyrgyzstan; Pennsylvania; Montana
- **uraninite**—Katanga; Ontario; southwestern United States
- **uraninite with zircon**—New Jersey
- **uranium**—Australia; Brazil; Canada; China; India; Jordan; Kazakhstan; Mongolia; Namibia; Niger; Russia; South Africa; Ukraine; United States

# Rocks

Rocks and minerals may look similar, but there is a distinct difference in their compositions. Rocks are composed of groups of minerals or of other rocks. Granite, for instance, is made up of several minerals—quartz, feldspar, and hornblende. Minerals are made of elements alone. Fluorite is composed of calcium fluoride, for instance, and diamonds are pure carbon.

Scientists who study minerals are called mineralogists, while those who study rocks and their origins are called petralogists. Both mineralogists and petralogists combine aspects of mineralogy, geology, chemistry, and physics in their studies. An amateur who collects rocks and minerals, especially one who hunts for them in their natural elements, is nicknamed "rock hound." An artisan who makes faceted jewelry from precious gem minerals goes by the name lapidary.

# The Birth of Rocks

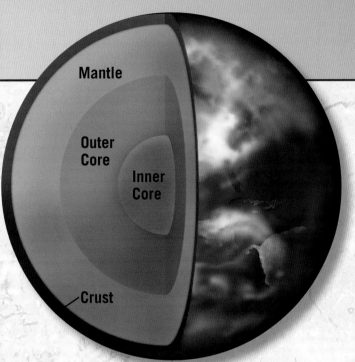

**W**hen the earth was young, it was a violent, white-hot world. Streams of magma—or superheated liquid rock—surged to the surface from the planet's interior. Water vapor and deadly gases rose into the atmosphere to block out the sun. During this phase, meteorites and cosmic dust bombarded the planet, increasing its size.

Millions of years passed before some of the magma cooled, leaving islands of solid lava in the fiery sea of molten rock. Scientists call the rocks formed by this volcanic activity *igneous*—from the Latin word for "fire."

## The Effects of Time

Over time, wind and water wore down many of those early rock formations into sediment—sand, gravel, and dust. (Think about this the next time you go to the beach—you're standing on tiny rocks that predate the dinosaurs.) Wind and water then deposited layers of sediment on the ground or in riverbeds, where the layers hardened, forming a porous type of rock called sedimentary, from the Latin word *sedimentum*, meaning, "settling." Sedimentary rocks make up roughly three-quarters of the earth's surface.

While nature's forces created sedimentary rock aboveground, pressure and heat beneath the earth's surface were forming a hard, dense rock called metamorphic, from the Greek word *metamorphosis*, meaning "transformation." Anywhere the earth's crust has been exposed—after earthquakes, during road excavations, or in quarries and canyons—you see layers of metamorphic rock, sometimes running at angles or even sideways to the other rock.

Diagram of the earth's layers. The outer layer, or crust, is composed of oxygen, magnesium aluminum, silicon calcium, sodium potassium, and iron and makes up less than 1 percent of the earth's mass (0.4 percent). The mantle, made of silicon, oxygen, aluminum, and iron, makes up about 70 percent. The iron core makes up 30 percent of the earth's mass.

## Earth's Layers

The earth consists of four layers: the inner core, the outer core, the mantle, and the crust. If you imagine the planet sliced in half, each layer would appear as a ring around the circular core.

- The inner core, made up of iron heated to 7,000°F (4,000°C), is approximately 1,500 miles (2,400 km) in diameter. Massive pressure keeps it in a solid state.

- The outer core is a mass of molten iron 1,475 miles (2,370 km) in width. It is here that electrical currents generate the earth's electromagnetic field.

- The mantle is a layer of rock 1,750 miles (2,800 km) wide. When this rock heats up, it forms the magma that surges to the surface in volcanoes.

- The crust, which is made up of rock and sand, varies from 4 miles to 25 miles (6–40 km) in thickness.

## The Rock Cycle

As eons pass, rocks constantly re-create themselves, changing from igneous to sedimentary to metamorphic and then back to igneous. This process, called the rock cycle, takes place as follows:

- After molten rock cools at or below the earth's surface, movement in the crust thrusts these igneous rock deposits into ridges or mountains.
- These upheavals are exposed to atmospheric erosion, creating sediment or soil. Wind and water carry away the sediments or soil and deposit them on the surface.

- As these deposits become compacted (lithified), they form sedimentary rocks.
- Pressure, temperature variations, and alterations in the chemistry of the rocks create metamorphic layers.
- When the metamorphic layers (or sedimentary layers) are subjected to enough heat, they become molten, or igneous, rocks, beginning the cycle once again.

The rock cycle. Over thousands and millions of years, natural processes, such as erosion and weathering, constantly form rocks, wear them down, and reform them.

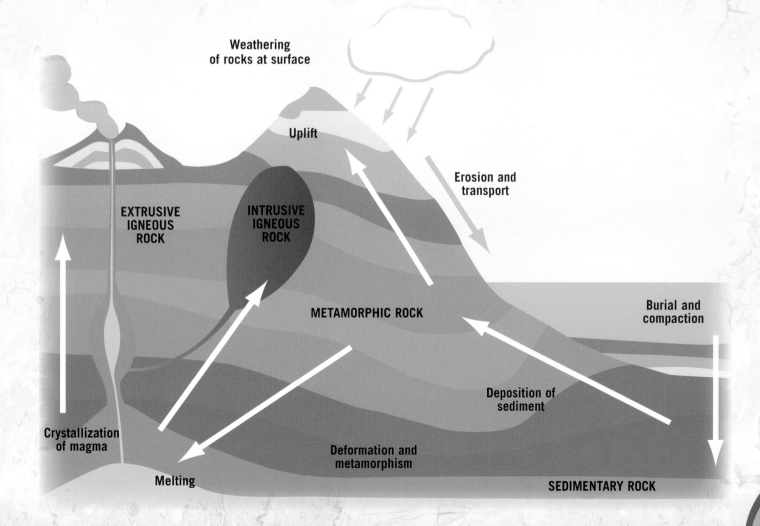

Weathering of rocks at surface

Uplift

Erosion and transport

EXTRUSIVE IGNEOUS ROCK

INTRUSIVE IGNEOUS ROCK

Burial and compaction

METAMORPHIC ROCK

Deposition of sediment

Crystallization of magma

Deformation and metamorphism

Melting

SEDIMENTARY ROCK

# Classification of Rocks

In addition to classifying rocks by how they are formed, scientists further classify them based on texture and composition. Texture refers to their level of graininess, and composition reflects their mineral content.

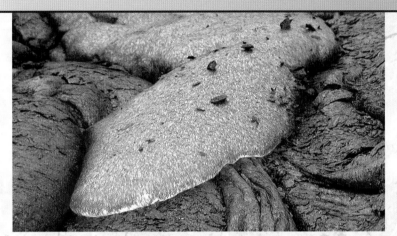

Over time, this glowing-hot basalt lava will form into solid rock formations.

### Texture

Scientists use the terms *phaneritic* ("coarse-grained") and *aphanitic* ("fine-grained") to describe the texture of all three rock types.

### Igneous Rocks

Scientists look at the size of a specimen's crystals and its texture when deciding if a rock is igneous.

This specimen of gabbro shows its coarse-grained, or phaneritic, texture.

- **Crystal size.** Scientists consider igneous rocks coarse grained if the grains are larger than 1/400 of an inch (1/16 mm). Slow-cooling intrusive rocks tend to be coarse, or phaneritic. Fast-cooling extrusive rocks are finer grained, or aphanitic, Slow-cooling rocks with high water content are called pegmatitic. Fast-cooling rocks with high silica content, such as obsidian, are called glassy. There is also two-phased cooling: slow cooling followed by fast cooling results in a fine-grained rock with distinct crystals. Very slow cooling followed by slow cooling creates a coarse-grained rock, also with distinct crystals. Basalt is an aphanitic igneous rock, and granite and gabbro are examples of phaneritic rocks.

- **Volcanic texture.** Volcanic texture is another way to identify igneous rocks. If the specimen once contained bubbles with low gas content, resulting in shallow pocks, or pits, the rock is considered vesicular or amygdaloidal. If there were lots of gas bubbles, resulting in the look of rocky foam, the rock is labeled pumice or scoria. If there was actual explosive debris in the rock, causing pits and craters, it is called pyroclastic.

### Sedimentary Rocks

Here, the difference between fine- and coarse-grained is 1/10,000 inch (1/256 mm). The texture of specimens breaks down by descending size into gravel (boulders, cobbles, pebbles, and granules), sand, silt, and clay.

### Metamorphic Rocks

Scientists describe metamorphic rocks as either nonfoliated (showing no layers) or, if there are visible layers, foliated.

Augen gneiss, a coarse-grained foliated metamorphic rock, shows its layering of quartz, biotite, and magnetite bands.

### Composition

Scientists categorize rocks by their mineral content. All three rock types have their own subcategories.

### Igneous Rocks

Scientists break down igneous rocks into four groups: mafic, ultramafic, felsic, and intermediate.

- Mafic rocks contain plagioclase and pyroxene with small amounts of olivine.
- Ultramafic rocks contain large amounts of olivine and/or pyroxene.
- Felsic rocks contain large amounts of feldspar, roughly 10 percent quartz, and less than 15 percent mafic minerals.
- Intermediate rocks contain a mix of felsic minerals, mainly plagioclase, and mafic minerals, such as hornblende, pyroxene, and biotite.

### Sedimentary Rocks

Scientists break down sedimentary rocks into three groups: clastic, carbonate, and evaporate.

- Clastic rocks, composed of silicate minerals such as quartz, feldspar, mica, and clay minerals, form from clay, silt, gravel, or boulders. Although coal, made of compressed plant debris, is not technically a clastic rock, it is often present in clastic deposits.
- Carbonate or organic rocks are generally made of the minerals calcite (which forms limestone) or dolomite (which forms dolostone). Shell material, called bioclastic debris, makes up many carbonate rocks.

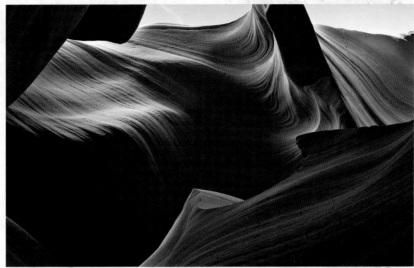

The striking interior of Lower Antelope Canyon, Arizona. The clastic sedimentary rock red sandstone, worn smooth by erosion from flash flooding over millions of years, forms the canyon walls.

- Evaporate rocks form when bodies of water dry up, creating the minerals gypsum and halite and the rocks of the same name.

### Metamorphic Rocks

Scientists break down metamorphic rocks into two groups: foliated and nonfoliated.

- Foliated (layered) metamorphic rocks owe their distinct layering to multiple minerals in their compositions—schist, for example, displays a mixture of mica, quartz, and feldspar. The three types of layering are described as slaty cleavage (which means that the rock tends to break along parallel lines), schistosity (it has visible crystals), and banding (the different minerals in the rock's layers form parallel bands).
- Nonfoliated metamorphic rocks are usually all one mineral; for example, marble is composed of calcite. Tiny impurities, rather than a variety of minerals, form the color bands in nonfoliated metamorphic rock.

# From Earth's Fiery Core

When molten rock, or magma, cools and solidifies, it forms igneous rock. If this cooling occurs below the surface, the rocks are called intrusive—or plutonic. When cooling occurs above the surface, the rocks are called extrusive—or volcanic.

Most igneous rocks are intrusive and make up 95 percent of the upper layer of the earth's crust. They lie below a thin layer of both metamorphic and sedimentary rocks. Within these deposits of metamorphic rocks lie valuable mineral ores, such as tin and uranium. Because the magma of intrusive rocks cools slowly, intrusive rocks are typically coarse grained.

Extrusive igneous rocks cool and crystallize quickly, so they are fine grained. Extremely rapid cooling results in rocks that are mostly glass, such as obsidian.

**Dikes crisscross the walls of the Black Canyon in Gunnison National Park in Colorado.**

## Intrusive Rock Structures

Intrusive rock deposits form distinct structures beneath the ground. Although these deposits are often deep below the surface, glaciers and erosion of the covering layers can expose them.

- Batholiths are the largest rock formations, often spreading over thousands of miles. A batholith beneath the state of Iowa measures 16,000 square miles (26,000 square km).

**The gigantic granite dome known as Half Dome, in Yosemite National Park, is part of the extensive batholith that forms the core of California's Sierra Nevada mountain range.**

- Dikes are sheetlike protrusions that rise out of batholiths or from other sources of magma, cutting across the existing layers of rock.
- Sills are similar to dikes, but they form parallel to existing rocks. The Palisades along the Hudson River in New Jersey and New York are a famous example of a sill.
- Laccoliths are similar in appearance to mushrooms. They occur when a narrow stream of magma pushes into an area and widens to form a broad, rounded deposit, often forcing the rock layers above it into a dome shape.

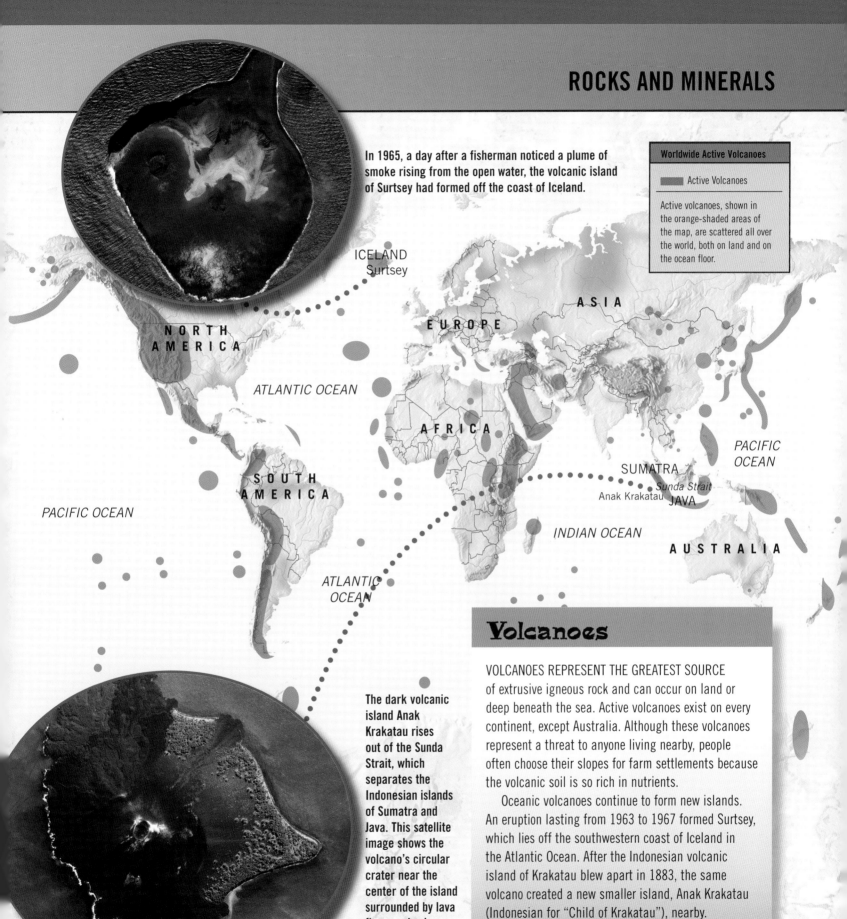

In 1965, a day after a fisherman noticed a plume of smoke rising from the open water, the volcanic island of Surtsey had formed off the coast of Iceland.

ICELAND
Surtsey

**Worldwide Active Volcanoes**

Active Volcanoes

Active volcanoes, shown in the orange-shaded areas of the map, are scattered all over the world, both on land and on the ocean floor.

ASIA

EUROPE

NORTH AMERICA

ATLANTIC OCEAN

AFRICA

PACIFIC OCEAN

SUMATRA
Sunda Strait
Anak Krakatau JAVA

PACIFIC OCEAN

SOUTH AMERICA

INDIAN OCEAN

AUSTRALIA

ATLANTIC OCEAN

The dark volcanic island Anak Krakatau rises out of the Sunda Strait, which separates the Indonesian islands of Sumatra and Java. This satellite image shows the volcano's circular crater near the center of the island surrounded by lava flows and ash.

## Volcanoes

VOLCANOES REPRESENT THE GREATEST SOURCE of extrusive igneous rock and can occur on land or deep beneath the sea. Active volcanoes exist on every continent, except Australia. Although these volcanoes represent a threat to anyone living nearby, people often choose their slopes for farm settlements because the volcanic soil is so rich in nutrients.

Oceanic volcanoes continue to form new islands. An eruption lasting from 1963 to 1967 formed Surtsey, which lies off the southwestern coast of Iceland in the Atlantic Ocean. After the Indonesian volcanic island of Krakatau blew apart in 1883, the same volcano created a new smaller island, Anak Krakatau (Indonesian for "Child of Krakatau"), nearby.

# Cooled Below the Surface

**D**iorite, gabbro, granite, pegmatite, and syenite all form by cooling below the earth's surface. These are often very common rocks, particularly granite and gabbro. In fact, granite is found all over the world, and it is even known as "Earth's Rock" because it is only found on our planet.

## Diorite

Diorite is a dull bluish gray or greenish intrusive rock, often with paler flecks. Plagioclase feldspar (andesine), biotite, hornblende, and/or pyroxene make up diorite, which is a mineral source of zircon, apatite, sphene, magnetite, and sulfides.

A specimen of diorite, showing pale flecks

## Diorite in Art

BECAUSE OF ITS EXTREME HARDNESS, diorite was a favorite tool of early artisans working in granite. They also used diorite as a base for carvings and inscriptions. Ancient Babylonians carved one famous example, the Code of Hammurabi, on a 7-foot (2.13 m) pillar (or stele) of black diorite. You can see the pillar on display in the Louvre Museum in Paris, France. Widely used by the ancient Egyptians, Assyrians, and Sumerians, diorite was so valued in Mesopotamia that military expeditions actually went in search of it. The Mayans and Incas used diorite in their fortresses, and it was a favorite building material in the Islamic world. Throughout medieval England, it was a popular cobblestone. The steps of St. Paul's Cathedral in London are made of diorite, polished by centuries of foot traffic.

The upper part of the Code of Hammurabi pillar, carved out of diorite

## What's in a Name?

Many places are proud of their granite heritage, earning themselves "rocking" nicknames.

- New Hampshire uses the nickname the Granite State.
- Barre, Vermont, boasts that it is the Granite Capital of the World.
- Elberton, Georgia, also calls itself the Granite Capital.
- Aberdeen, Scotland, goes by the name the Granite City.

## Gabbro

Gabbro, named after a town in Tuscany, Italy, is a dark, coarse-grained intrusive rock, chemically identical to basalt (an extrusive rock). It is composed of pyroxene, plagioclase feldspar, amphibole, and olivine. Much of the earth's surface is composed of gabbro, which lies beneath the oceanic crust. Gabbro contains valuable deposits of chromium, nickel, cobalt, gold, silver, platinum, and copper sulfides. Builders cover building facades with gabbro and line walkways with gabbro paving stones. Manufacturers sell it under the name "black granite" for constructing burial headstones and kitchen countertops.

## Granite

One of the most common intrusive rocks, granite has a medium to coarse texture, which accounts for its name, from the Latin *granum*, or "grain." It is composed largely of the minerals potash feldspar and quartz, with traces of mica and hornblende. Granite is technically a "massive" rock—meaning it lacks internal structure—and often forms the foundation of mountain chains. Its toughness and durability make it ideal for the construction of large buildings and monuments. It occurs in shades ranging from pink to gray and black and is quite beautiful when polished. Granite often contains gemstones, such as tourmaline, beryl, topaz, zircon, and apatite.

## DID YOU KNOW?

The United States' first railroad was built to haul granite from quarries in Quincy, Massachusetts. But perhaps the oddest use of granite was as rails for the Haytor Granite Tramway in Devon, England.

**Pegmatite containing lepidolite, tourmaline, and quartz**

## Pegmatite

Pegmatite is a pale, very coarse-grained intrusive rock, noted for its large—sometimes gigantic—crystals. Quartz, feldspar and mica make up pegmatite, which often contains deposits of rare earth minerals as well as aquamarine, beryl, tourmaline, topaz, fluorite, and apatite. Tin and tungsten have been mined from pegmatite, and it is a major source of the element lithium and of beryllium.

## Syenite

Course-grained syenite is similar in composition to granite, but lacks any significant quantities of quartz. The name syenite came from Syene, Egypt, and was originally applied to hornblende granite.

## Porphyry

Porphyries are shallow intrusive or extrusive rocks that contain visible crystals set in a finer, glassy base, or matrix. You can identify porphyry by its matrix content, such as granite porphyry. The name comes from the Greek word meaning "purple." The Romans used a brownish purple form of the rock, which they called imperial porphyry, to construct buildings and monuments.

**Remnants of the Haytor Granite Tramway, which carried granite down from the Haytor Down quarry in Devon to a canal 10 miles (16 km) below**

**At left, a yellow-flecked specimen of rust-colored porphyry. Although its name means "purple," porphyry comes in a variety of colors.**

# Cooled Above the Surface

Dome rocks, such as basalt, obsidian, pumice, and rhyolite, cool above the earth's surface, sometimes forming into distinct shapes or displaying sleek, glasslike textures.

## Basalt

Basalt is a dense, dark volcanic rock that occurs worldwide. It is composed of pyroxene and plagioclase feldspar, though in such a fine mixture that neither mineral is visible. It sometimes weathers to a limy gray in dry climates or a rusty red in humid locations. Basalt that cooled at the surface of basaltic flows sometimes contains gas bubbles, creating a porous, cindery rock called scoria. If the almond-shaped pockets in the rock later filled up with minerals, such as agate or amethyst, the rock is called amygdaloidal basalt. These basalts are a source of copper ore.

The Giant's Causeway curves from the sloping coast of County Antrim into the North Channel between Northern Ireland and Scotland.

## Obsidian

When lava cools very quickly, the result is a form of translucent natural glass called obsidian. American Indians fashioned knives, arrowheads, and ornaments from obsidian.

Obsidian is often black or a deep root-beer brown.

## ROCK STARS
### Giant's Causeway

ON IRELAND'S NORTHEAST COAST lies the Giant's Causeway, a magnificent example of an extrusive rock sill. Composed of basalt, the 36-foot-high (10 m) natural stockade of 40,000 columns formed when an eruption of magma flowed through a chalk base. As the magma rapidly cooled, horizontal contractions created a network of fractures resulting in the interlocking columns. The top of the Causeway forms a surface like paving stones and reveals the hexagonal, or six-sided, shape of many of the columns.

Irish folklore claims that legendary giant Fionn McCool built the Causeway to walk to Scotland in order to battle his enemy Banandonner. Similar basalt formations include Fingal's Cave in Scotland; Jusangjeolli on Jeju Island, South Korea; the Garni Gorge in Armenia; the Cyclopean Isles near Sicily; Devil's Postpile in California; the Cove Palisades in Oregon; Devil's Tower in Wyoming; Santa Maria Regla Basalt Prisms in Hidalgo, Mexico; the Organ Pipes on Mount Cargill in New Zealand; and the giant *Rocha dos Bordões* ("Rock of the Pilgrims' Staffs") formation on Flores Island in the Atlantic Ocean.

A line of *moai* look out toward the sea. Their builders transported hundreds of the big-headed statues to the perimeter of Rapa Nui, where they set them on stone platforms called *ahu*.

## Pumice

When the heated gases in lava create a spongelike froth that cools quickly, pumice forms. It is composed of glass with many tiny cavities and thin bubble walls of volcanic rock.

## Rhyolite

Rhyolite is a pale, fine-textured volcanic rock, similar in composition to granite. It can range in color from white to pink to gray. Rhyolite can also form variations of pumice and obsidian.

## ROCK STARS
### Rapa Nui

FAR OFF THE COAST OF CHILE lies remote Rapa Nui (also known as Easter Island), home to the Rapanui people. This Pacific Ocean island is famous for its 887 big-headed stone statues called *moai*, which were used in ancestor worship ceremonies. The Polynesian colonizers of the island carved the *moai* between circa 1250 and 1500 CE. They sculpted most of the moai, which can weigh up to 82 tons (74 mt), from a compressed volcanic ash, or tuff, taken from inside the crater of the extinct volcano Rano Raraku.

# Creations of Wind and Water

Stromatolites form in shallow water when microorganisms, such as blue-green algae, bind with sedimentary grains. These rock formations were once abundant all over the planet, but few remain, such as this one in Shark's Bay, Western Australia.

Sedimentary rocks are remarkable for their varied colors, textures, and composition. The forces of weather—wind and water—or chemical reactions create them. In either case, millions of years of erosion wore down exposed igneous rock formations, creating small particles that air currents carried away. Many of these tiny fragments ended up in streambeds, where they were washed into rivers, lakes, and oceans. A process called lithification compressed this massive buildup of rock particles (otherwise known as silt or mud) until, over time, sedimentary rock formed.

## A Thin Crust

Sedimentary rocks, including chalk, conglomerate, dolomite, limestone, sandstone, and shale, make up between 75 and 80 percent of the exposed land on Earth, but only as a thin veneer on the surface. Overall, sedimentary rocks make up a scant 5 percent of the planet's rocks.

### Layers of History

Sedimentary rocks are typically laid down in layers, or strata, with newer layers forming over older ones. This sandwiching effect allows scientists to study the earth's history because the mineral composition of each stratum can reveal a great deal about the climate and conditions of that particular era. Sedimentary layers also contain fossils, preserved plant and animal remains, giving scientists a glimpse of life on the planet at the time that the fossilized species actually lived.

### Classification of Sedimentary Rocks

There are three types of sedimentary rocks—carbonate, chemical, and clastic—named according to how they were formed.

#### Carbonate

These sedimentary rocks were created from the remains of living organisms. The calcite in mollusks, corals, and plankton skeletons form the organic rocks that originated in the ocean, such as limestone. Stromatolites and flint nodes in chalk are organic in origin, as are coal and oil shale, which are composed of the compressed remains of tropical plants.

#### Chemical

These rocks, also called evaporate rocks, formed when the minerals in a rock were chemically altered. If a sedimentary formation lay beneath a shrinking ocean, for instance, over time, evaporation would affect the minerals in the rock. Chemical rocks include limonite, dolomite, and oolitic hematite, as well the evaporate minerals barite, gypsum, halite, and sylvite.

Dramatic sandstone rock formations at Drumheller, in Alberta, Canada. Natural forces work on sedimentary rocks to carve out some of the world's most amazing landscapes.

#### Clastic

These are grainy rocks formed from fragments—or clasts—of other rocks, with quartz as their main component. Two types of weathering—mechanical and chemical—are responsible for their formation. Mechanical weathering leaves the mineral content of the rock intact, while chemical weathering alters the minerals, making the rock particles blow away more easily.

### Salting the Roads

DURING THE WINTER in colder climates, highway departments and homeowners use halite, or rock salt, to clear away ice. But, why does rock salt dissolve ice? It's because saline (a mixture of salt and water) has a lower freezing point than plain water. So, when you throw rock salt onto ice, saline forms—causing the ice to begin melting immediately.

**Anthracite. This black rock supplies us with "lead" for our pencils and charcoal for our barbecue grills.**

**A brooch made of polished jet. After the death of her husband, Prince Albert, Queen Victoria of England made wearing this inky black stone popular when she chose it for mourning jewelry.**

## Coal

Coal is an organic sedimentary rock, although harder varieties, such as anthracite, can be classified as metamorphic. Coal deposits formed when dead plant life was prevented from biodegrading by water or mud. Fuel coals range in density from peat and lignite (brown coal) to subbituminous and bituminous to glossy black anthracite. Graphite, which is used in making pencils and as a lubricant, is also a form of coal. Worldwide, coal is the most commonly used fuel for producing electricity, though it is also a major air pollutant.

## Conglomerates

Conglomerates look like a handful of pebbles held together by smaller grains of rock. They generally form at the mouth of rivers with calcium carbonate, silica, iron oxide, or clay binding them together.

The pebbles, which can sometimes be as large as boulders, are most often quartz or quartzite. Conglomerates with rough, jagged edges are called breccia and are usually found close to their pebbles' sources of origin.

**Breccia, made of dolomite (light gray), jasperoid (dark gray), and quartz (white)**

## Dolomite Rock, or Dolostone

These sedimentary rocks contain high concentrations of the mineral dolomite. French mineralogist Déodat de Dolomieu first described dolomite rock in 1791, while exploring the southern Alps in Italy. Today, that entire mountain range is known as the Dolomites. Dolomite rock, also called dolostone, forms white or pink crystals, and, because it is porous, underground deposits often contain petroleum. It is also used as an ornamental stone and is a source for lead, zinc, and copper ore.

## WEARING COAL

People have polished and worn jet, a compact form of lignite, since the Iron Age (1200–550 BCE). Both the Egyptians and the Pueblo Indians considered it a protection in the afterlife, and Roman Catholics in European began carving jet into rosary beads in the sixteenth century. To today's New Age practitioners, it is known as the travelers' amulet.

**This sample of dolomite shows the formation of large white crystals.**

### Shale

Shale is simply clay that has hardened into rock. It is usually gray, but its color ranges from deep red to black. The dark and light layers of lake shale are called varves, with a pair of layers forming each year. The layers helps scientists to age deposits. Shale is used to manufacture cement and, in the case of some varieties, as oil reservoirs for when other sources have been used up.

Cannonball concretions, such as this one on the coast of Greenland (at center), are huge, but other cannonballs are closer in size to their namesake.

Moqui marble

# CONCRETIONS: ODDBALL ROCKS

Imagine a rock that looks like a cannonball or a walnut or even a highway map. These are some of the shapes or patterns produced by concretions—mineral deposits that formed inside hollows in sedimentary rock, usually before the sediment had fully hardened. The term *concretion* comes from the Latin for "to grow together."

- **Moqui marbles**—Found in sandstone outcroppings in Utah, these iron-oxide concretions range in shape from balls, disks, and buttons to spiked spheres and walnuts.

- **Kansas pop rocks**—These pocket-sized concretions of iron sulfide or jarosite got their name because they will explode if thrown into a fire.

- **cannonballs**—These large, round calcite concretions, some reaching 18 feet (5.5 m) in diameter, can be found in North Dakota, Utah, Wyoming, and Kansas, as well as New Zealand, Greenland, and Canada. They typically appear on eroded outcroppings.

- **septarian nodules**—These richly veined or patterned concretions were possibly formed by the dehydration of clay-rich cores, earthquakes, expansion of gases, or shrinkage of a concretion's center. Large examples, up to 9 feet (2.7 m), called the Moeraki Boulders, litter the coastline of New Zealand. Smaller examples lie along the Wessex coast of England.

At left, looking like turtles sunning on the beach, the Moeraki Boulders lie along the New Zealand coastline.

Kansas pop rock

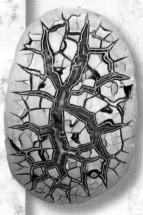

Septarian nodule

The mineral gypsum composes the sedimentary rock gypsum, which tends to form in desert lakes and marine areas with high evaporation rates.

### Gypsum

The evaporate rock gypsum comes in many forms: crystalline, silky and fibrous, granular, or compact. Deposits form in lakes, seawater, and hot springs, and from volcanic vapor. A large quarry outside Paris, France, furnished so much burnt gypsum that the substance became known as plaster of paris. Rock gypsum has been used as a wood substitute, for surgical splints and casting molds, in drywall, as blackboard chalk, as a binder in tennis court clay, and as a thickener of tofu (soybean curds). Masons also use it to prevent cement from drying too quickly.

### Limestone

Limestone appears in a variety of colors and textures, and is typically made up of the mineral calcite, the result of marine creatures decomposing and leaving their calcium-rich skeletons behind. Limestone

It may look like cascading snow, but that is solid rock. Deposits of limestone build up over millions of years, molding the landscape into fantastic shapes and forms.

can range in composition from a loose conglomeration of visible shells (called coquina) to compacted crystalline rocks similar to marble. Limestone is used in concrete, as a building stone, and as a source for garden lime.

### Sandstone

Sandstone is composed of small grains of the minerals quartz and feldspar cemented by lime, silica, or iron oxide. Most sandstone deposits formed in coastal areas beneath shallow seas and show fossil remains of mollusks. Sandstone frequently occurs in attractive layers, making it a popular material for ornamental buildings and monuments.

## ROCK STARS
### A Surprise Inside

A GEODE IS A DULL-COLORED BALL of rock that comes with a built-in surprise. When you split it in half, it reveals a beautiful crystal-lined hollow. This rock cavity, or vug, forms inside gas bubbles in igneous rock or inside rounded cavities in sedimentary rock. If dissolved silicates or carbonates have coated the interior walls, over time, trickling water can cause crystals of quartz or chalcedony to grow. If a geode's crystal center is solid, it is called a nodule. Thunder eggs resemble solid geodes and are formed by rhyolitic lava flows.

## ROCK STARS
### Lost Treasures

TWO OF THE UNITED STATES' best-known rock formations recently lost their battles with gravity and erosion. The first to go was the Old Man of the Mountain—or Great Stone Face—a craggy granite face looming above Profile Lake in Franconia Notch, New Hampshire. In 2003, the famous face shattered and fell into the valley below. The Old Man's image is the state emblem of New Hampshire and appears on its license plate; it is also on the reverse of the New Hampshire state quarter and was honored with a U.S. postage stamp and reproduced on thousands of souvenirs.

In 2008, one of the largest stone arches in Arches National Park in Utah collapsed. Composed of entrada sandstone and more than 33 feet (10 m) high, Wall Arch on the Devil's Garden Trail had been a favorite with photographers.

Wall Arch, above, just weeks before it collapsed. The inset shows the Old Man in the Mountain's jagged profile in a photo taken just six days before the face tumbled into the lake below. Although it is hard to lose such natural treasures, rocks are constantly forming, crumbling, and re-forming.

# Nature's Rock Gardens

**A**lthough the forces of weathering help create sedimentary rock deposits, they are also responsible for breaking them down again in an ongoing cycle. Fortunately, many of these weathered rocks formations possess a striking beauty appreciated by photographers and sightseers.

**Flowerpot Formations, Georgian Bay, Ontario**
Georgian Bay is home to Flowerpot Island, which took its name from high pillars with flowerpot-shaped tops. Waves in the bay gradually eroded the limestone bases into the "pots."

NORTH AMERICA

ATLANTIC OCEAN

AFRI

**Bryce Canyon Hoodoos, Utah**
One of Utah's most scenic destinations, Bryce Canyon features endless variations of sedimentary forms. Wind, ice, and water erosion created these tall, slender, minaret-shaped hoodoos.

SOUTH AMERICA

**Eroded Sandstone, Monument Valley National Park, Arizona and Utah**
Wind easily sculpts soft sandstone—with dramatic results.

PACIFIC OCEAN

ATLANTIC OCEAN

**The Grand Canyon, Arizona**
Major John Wesley Powell, who made the first recorded journey along the length of the canyon in 1869, described the colorful layers of sandstone revealed by erosion as "leaves in a great storybook."

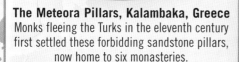

**The Meteora Pillars, Kalambaka, Greece**
Monks fleeing the Turks in the eleventh century first settled these forbidding sandstone pillars, now home to six monasteries.

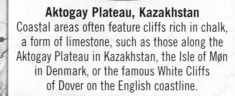

**Aktogay Plateau, Kazakhstan**
Coastal areas often feature cliffs rich in chalk, a form of limestone, such as those along the Aktogay Plateau in Kazakhstan, the Isle of Møn in Denmark, or the famous White Cliffs of Dover on the English coastline.

EUROPE

*PACIFIC OCEAN*

ASIA

**Coquina Outcroppings, Florida**
*Coquina,* Spanish for "cockle," is a limestone conglomerate composed of seashells and coral, and early European settlers of the area used it for building. Coquina helped protect the walls of the Castillo de San Marcos, the fort at St. Augustine, because cannonballs would simply sink into the soft surface.

*INDIAN OCEAN*

**Weka Pass Formation Limestone, Kaikoura, New Zealand**
These distinctive limestone rocks, located in southern New Zealand, offer a vivid example of compressing and folding with high cleavage.

**Uluru, Alice Springs, Australia**
Also known as Ayers Rock, this sandstone "island mountain" in Australia's outback stands 1,142 feet (348 m) high and is 5.8 miles (9.3 km) in circumference. Uluru, the last remnant of an eroded mountain range, is sacred to the local aboriginal people.

AUSTRALIA

# Imprints of the Past

Fossils are the preserved remains or imprints of organisms that lived thousands, or even millions of years ago. When most plants or animals die, scavengers and bacteria consume them until they become compost. Yet, sometimes, the organism does not decompose.

## Types of Fossils

Fossils form in a number of ways. Some animals freeze whole in arctic ice, others mummify, or dry up and shrivel—in peat bogs, for instance. Paleontologists, scientists who study fossils, have even discovered mummies with their tissues still intact. Others animals are trapped in tar (asphalt) or preserved in pine resin (amber).

Two rock-related methods of preservation are carbonization and permineralization. In carbonization, the most common method of fossil preservation, the remains of a plant or animal decompose, except for the

Layers in this sedimentary rock section from Morocco reveal a treasure trove of marine fossils.

Millions of years ago, this ancient frog became trapped in pine resin, which eventually turned into amber.

carbon, which leaves a distinct impression in the rock. In permineralization, liquid minerals replace organic tissue, which then crystallize. After crystallization takes place, most—or all—of the original organism has turned to rock.

Trace fossils form geological records of animal activity, such as footprints of prehistoric creatures that were preserved in mud or silt that hardened to rock. Casts occur when minerals fill the hollowed-out areas.

## How a Fossil Forms

1. The organism must die in or near water.
2. Sedimentation must occur quickly, covering and protecting the remains.
3. Sediment continues to build up above the remains, creating pressure that turns the lower layers to rock.
4. Mineral-rich water filters through the sediment, sometimes for millions of years.
5. Minerals that replicate the exact shape of the organism replace molecules of the original organism.
6. Tectonic plate movement, or the shifting of the earth's crust, lifts seafloors and lakebeds closer to the surface.
7. Erosion wears away the layers above the fossil, making it easier for scientists and rock hounds to find.

## FOSSILS TO COLLECT

These are some of the more common fossils that are available in rock stores, museum shops, and online. Adventurous fossil hunters can search in areas where sedimentary layers have been exposed: highway cuts, eroded hillsides, quarries, and riverbanks.

### Ammonites

Ammonites were cephalopods (the same mollusk class as squid and octopuses) with ram's horn–shaped shells, similar in appearance to the modern chambered nautilus. They filled the seas for 300 million years but became extinct 65 million years ago, likely from the same mysterious worldwide cataclysm that killed off the dinosaurs.

**Ammonite**

### Brachiopods

Brachiopods, bivalves unrelated to clams or other mollusks, still exist today, though not in the numbers seen during the Paleozoic era (542–251 million years ago), when they covered the seafloor. They are possibly the most numerous fossils on the planet.

**Brachiopod**

### Crinoids

Crinoids, starfishlike marine animals, are also still thriving in the oceans. They represent some of the oldest fossils, going back at least to the Ordovician period, more than 400 million years ago.

**Crinoid**

### Fern and Plant Imprints

Fern and plant imprint fossils can go back more than 400 million years and are found in both tropic and temperate zones.

**Fossil fern**

### Orthoceras

Orthoceras was a primitive mollusk with a long, conical shell and feet that grew out of its head. It lived 400 million years ago and is an ancestor of the squid.

**Orthoceras**

### Megalodon

Megalodon, which roamed the seas from 16 to 2 million years ago, was a prehistoric shark that grew to 50 feet (15 m) in length. Although shark skeletons are made of cartilage and rarely fossilize, megalodon teeth fossils are readily available to collectors.

**Megalodon**

### Petrified Wood

Petrified wood, which is collected for its beautiful colors and texture, retains the appearance of the original tree trunk or branch after mineralization has occurred.

### Trilobites

Trilobites were early armored arthropods, from the same phylum as spiders, ants, and lobsters. They arose in the seas 450 million years ago and lasted for nearly 300 million years. The best fossils clearly show the trilobites' segmented exoskeletons and jointed legs

**Petrified wood**

**Trilobites**

# Under Pressure and Taking Heat

When an existing rock type, called the protolith, changes in form or structure it becomes a metamorphic rock. Igneous, sedimentary, and older metamorphic rocks can all undergo physical and chemical changes caused by pressure or heat. Often the rock develops a new crystalline structure. Because water plays an important role in the creation of metamorphic rocks, many of them contain elements that were not present in the original rock.

## Metamorphism

This process can take place deep within the earth, due to the great heat and pressure from above that exists there. Or, it can occur during the shifting of continental tectonic plates, when horizontal pressure transforms the rock. The intrusion of molten magma can also heat up existing rock and change its form.

By studying metamorphic rocks that have been thrust up to the surface, scientists can learn a great deal about what's going on deep below the earth's crust.

## Types of Metamorphism

Metamorphic rocks undergo three major types of changes: contact, dynamic, and regional metamorphism.

- Contact metamorphism occurs due to increase in temperature with little pressure or stress. It usually produces fine-grained rocks, such as hornfels.
- Dynamic metamorphism is the result of stresses that cause deformation or strain on the rock that involves little or no long-term temperature change. Dynamically altered rocks are largely developed in mountain belts, such as the Rocky Mountains. These rocks can range from jagged to fine grained or powdery.
- Regional metamorphism, which also occurs in mountain ranges, is a result of increases in both temperature and pressure taking place over a large area.

There are other types of metamorphism, including retrograde (mineral response to decrease in temperature or pressure); metasomatism (resulting from the addition or subtraction of components of the original rock); and hydrothermal (changes occurring from water at high temperatures or from water pressure).

The three major forms of metamorphism: contact, dynamic, and regional

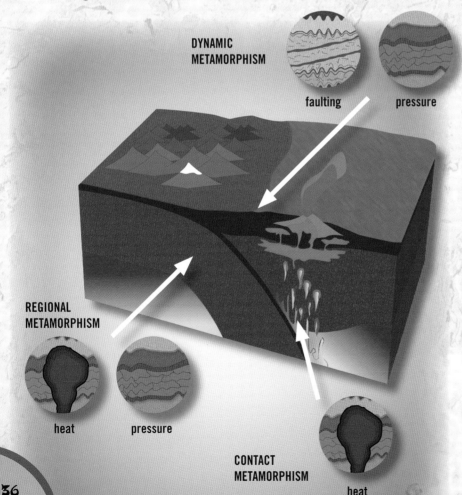

DYNAMIC METAMORPHISM

faulting

pressure

REGIONAL METAMORPHISM

heat

pressure

CONTACT METAMORPHISM

heat

## Metamorphic Rock Textures

Foliation is the name given to the layering found in some metamorphic rocks.

Foliation occurs when pressure occurs in one direction, causing minerals in the rock to grow perpendicular to the source of pressure. Rocks with evenly placed pressure show no foliation.

## Foliated Rocks

### Gneiss

Gneiss can be simple or complex, depending on the number of rocks in its origin. When gneiss is invaded by igneous materials it is called migmatite. Scientists classify gneiss by its source (granite gneiss), most prevalent mineral (hornblende gneiss), or by its structure (injection gneiss).

Schist stones from the Otago River in New Zealand

### Schist

Schist forms from phyllite under pressure and shows greater foliation due to the chlorine and mica again increasing in size. Schists are named for their predominant mineral, as in mica schist and hornblende schist, for example.

### Slate

The metamorphosis of shale or basalt forms slate, which is usually a blue-gray color, though it sometimes occurs in shades of green, red, or brown. It is used for roofing and flagstones.

Slate

Gneiss

### Phyllite

Phyllite is formed from slate, when pressure causes chlorine and mica crystals to increase in size. This gives some phyllite a wavy appearance when viewed from the side.

Phyllite

# Under Pressure and Taking Heat

**Nonfoliated Rocks**

Hornfels

### *Hornfels*
Hornfels is a form of metamorphosed shale, or clay, created by the heat of igneous rocks. Typically a dark, dense stone, hornfels is a source for garnet and other semiprecious minerals.

### *Marble*
Marble is a massive rock that formed from limestone when its calcite crystals began to fuse together. Although limestone usually appears white, tiny impurities in the source limestone give marble varying colors. Marble is beautiful when polished, and because it is only a 3.5 on the Mohs scale, it is easy to work with and is used for building, monuments, sculpture, and countertops.

Marble

### *Metaconglomerate*
This is the high-grade metamorphosed version of conglomerate. In this rock, all the pebbles and grains within the original conglomerate flatten and stretch out as they are recrystallized. Zircons mined from metaconglomerates in the Jack Hills of Australia date back 4.4 billion years.

Metaconglomerate

Quartzite

### *Quartzite*
Quartzite forms when extreme heat causes the quartz grains in sandstone to fuse together, creating a hard, very durable rock. Pure quartzite is pale, but it also occurs in a number of deeper colors. It can be identified by its "sugary" surface.

### *Skarn*
Skarn occurs in the contact zone between carbonate rocks, such as limestone or dolostone, and magmatic intrusions, such as granite. Skarn deposits are valuable sources of lead, tin, copper, iron, and gold ores.

Skarn

# New York City Rocks

THE NEW YORK CITY BOROUGH of Manhattan lies above two massive bedrock formations of mica schist. This strong, durable rock makes the ideal foundation for skyscrapers. If you look at the city skyline, at the two areas with the largest clusters of tall buildings—in the lower and north-central parts of the island, you can tell where the Manhattan schist is closest to the surface, allowing deep excavation. Another bedrock layer, Fordham gneiss, lies under the Bronx.

New York City, known for its towering skyscrapers, sits on a solid foundation of mica schist (see inset photo). The Hartland Formation supplies the base for the midtown skyscrapers, shown above. Manhattan schist sits at various depths: from 18 feet (5.5 m) below the surface in Times Square, at the center of the island, to 260 feet (80 m) below in Greenwich Village, at the island's southern end. The lower group of skyscrapers is just visible at the top right of the photo.

# Monumental Structures

**Marble House, Newport, Rhode Island**
Designed by Beaux Arts architect Richard Morris Hunt, William Vanderbilt's lavish vacation "cottage" required 500,000 cubic feet (14,160 cubic m) of white marble. Hunt drew his inspiration from the Temple of the Sun at Heliopolis, Greece, and the Petit Trianon at Versailles, France.

From ancient times to the present day, builders have fashioned rock into amazing structures that can last for hundreds, and even thousands of years.

*ATLANTIC OCEAN*

NORTH AMERICA

**The Lincoln Memorial, Washington, D.C.**
This memorial to Abraham Lincoln, the fallen 16th president of the United States, was constructed of pure white Colorado Yule marble. Unfortunately, air and rain pollution have given parts of the exterior a worn "sugared" effect.

**The Colosseum, Rome, Italy**
This triumph of Roman engineering, built in the first century CE, was originally called the Flavian Amphitheater. The outer wall of the elliptical arena was constructed of travertine stone, using iron clamps instead of mortar.

*PACIFIC OCEAN*

SOUTH AMERICA

**Pyramid at Chichén-Itzá, Mexico**
The famous Kukulkan pyramid of Chichén-Itzá, built by the Maya civilization more than 1,500 years ago, is located in the northern center of the Yucatán Peninsula in present-day Mexico. The stepped-stone structure stands approximately 75 feet (23 m) tall.

**Timbuktu, Mali**
This fabled African city was a prosperous center of commerce and culture—and an important trading post for rock salt—during the fifteenth and sixteenth centuries. Many of Timbuktu's early buildings still stand today, including three great mosques made from hardened mud.

**Stonehenge, Wiltshire, England**
Dating back to approximately 2400 BCE, Stonehenge features a circle of towering blue stones hewn from Ordovician dolerite. Scholars once thought Stonehenge's builders transported the stones from distant Wales, but they now theorize that the Irish Sea glacier left them near the site.

**The Parthenon, Athens, Greece**
The Parthenon, built in white marble as a temple to Athena in the fifth century BCE, is the most important surviving example of classical Greek style. A roof originally covered the Parthenon, but it suffered catastrophic damage in 1687 when a stash of gunpowder stored in the temple exploded.

EUROPE

ASIA

PACIFIC OCEAN

AFRICA

INDIAN OCEAN

**The Great Wall of China**
Built between the fifth and sixteenth centuries CE, the Great Wall stretches more than 4,000 miles (6,437 km) across central China. Builders used local-cut stones for most of the foundation, while the walls were a combination of rock, brick, and packed earth.

**The Pyramids of Egypt**
For many centuries, the largest human-made structures in the world, the Pyramids were erected to protect the remains of the pharaohs. Though scholars believe the Pyramids were built of local limestone, new research indicates that some of the massive blocks were made from an early form of limestone concrete.

AUSTRALIA

**The Taj Mahal, Agra, India**
Built by Emperor Shah Jahan to honor his beloved wife, Mumutz Mahal, many people consider the marble-inlaid Taj Mahal to be the most beautiful building in the world.

# Minerals

**U**nlike rocks, minerals are homogeneous. This means that they are made up of only one thing—an element, such as gold or copper, or a combination of elements—and they will always be made of those particular elements in the form of a chemical compound. All minerals, regardless of their appearance, have a crystalline structure.

The composition of minerals can be simple—as with pure elements—or quite complex—as with silicates, which have thousands of forms. A mineral's internal crystalline structure, the orderly geometric arrangement of its atoms, determines its physical properties. Two minerals can have the same elemental makeup, but look different. Graphite and diamond are both pure carbon, yet, one is soft, and the other is the hardest mineral. The difference is how their atoms are arranged. Other minerals that look quite similar, especially clear, cubic specimens, can have completely different chemical compositions.

Minerals fall into four groups: metallic minerals, nonmetallic minerals, rock-forming minerals, and gem minerals.

# Precious Metallic Minerals

**M**ost valued of all the metallic minerals, these rare precious metals include the elements gold, palladium, platinum, and silver. Precious metals are less chemically reactive than other metals and are easier to work with, yet they have higher melting points. Historically, they have been used as currency, in jewelry, and in art.

## Gold

Gold has captured the human imagination since prehistoric times. The members of the earliest civilizations used it to adorn themselves and their temples, and over the passing centuries, gold has never lost its appeal—or its luster. Gold is unique among metallic minerals for its stability. It does not oxidize like copper or aluminum, it doesn't tarnish like silver, and it doesn't rust in water like iron. The gold jewelry archaeologists found in 4,000-year-old Egyptian tombs is still as bright as the day it was made.

A nugget of gold. Found in streams and other watercourses, gold nuggets are never pure gold. Most gold nuggets contain either silver or copper.

## Bullion

PRECIOUS METALS IN BULK FORM are known as bullion, which is how they are traded on the stock market. "Pure" bullion (which is 99.9 percent pure) can be melted into bars, called ingots, or made into coins for collectors and investors. The U.S. gold reserve, upon which the nation's currency is based, is stored in the form of ingots at the United States Bullion Depository in Fort Knox, Kentucky, and at the Federal Reserve Bank in New York City.

Gold ingots

## Golden Industry

Gold is also the most malleable metal, which means that it is easy to shape, even with primitive tools. You can hammer a single ounce so thin that it will form a 300-square-foot (28 square m) sheet. When it is beaten thin enough to see through, it is called gold leaf, which has been used to

## Gold Rush

WHEN GOLD DEPOSITS ERODE, the heavy nuggets often collect in streambeds. In the past, all it took was for one person to discover a few nuggets, and soon hundreds of gold prospectors would flock to that area. Major gold rushes took place in Alaska, California, and Australia, turning tiny settlements into boomtowns—until the gold ran out.

adorn manuscripts, capitol domes, and even birthday cakes. Primarily used in jewelry, gold is also a highly efficient conductor of heat and electricity. The electronics industry, medicine, space technology, and glass making all use gold.

## Palladium

Discovered in 1803, palladium is a silvery white precious metal used for jewelry. It has similar industrial applications to platinum and is used in electronics, as well as in carbon-monoxide detectors.

In recent years, palladium, above, has become increasingly popular with jewelers, who craft engagement rings, wedding bands, and other pieces out of this high-shine metal.

## Platinum

This lustrous silvery white metal, also primarily used for fine jewelry, is 30 times rarer than gold and often costs much more per ounce. Platinum does not oxidize, and it is a catalyst for chemical reactions. Technological industries utilize it for this quality, for instance, in building the catalytic converter in automobiles. Platinum is also used to refine crude petroleum into gasoline.

## Silver

Silver's value is based on its high-sheen beauty and its many practical uses. Though slightly harder than gold, silver is also easy to work. It has been used in jewelry, coins, and for eating utensils throughout history. In modern times, silver is used in electronics, dentistry, photography, as a solder, in batteries, and as control rods in nuclear reactors.

A shiny forint, a coin from Hungary, right, shows the beauty of polished silver, which is hard to see in dull bits of silver ore, above.

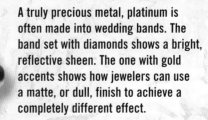

A truly precious metal, platinum is often made into wedding bands. The band set with diamonds shows a bright, reflective sheen. The one with gold accents shows how jewelers can use a matte, or dull, finish to achieve a completely different effect.

# The Core of Industry

Certain metallic minerals form the basis of our civilization. Without them, industry, science, medicine, and technology could never have advanced.

## Aluminum

Although silvery white aluminum is the most abundant metal in the earth's crust, it is always found combined with other minerals. It was not until the late nineteenth century that scientists found a way to extract a volume of pure aluminum from aluminum oxide and from bauxite. Today, the strong, lightweight metal is used for cans, foils, utensils, and in the construction of parts for jets and rockets. Major ore deposits lie in Ghana, Indonesia, Jamaica, Russia, and Surinam. Aluminum is 100 percent recyclable.

## Chromium

This hard, lustrous metal, which is highly resistant to oxidation, is a key component of stainless steel (along with iron and nickel) and is also used in electroplating.

Chromium electroplating, or coating another metal in a thin, continuous film of chrome, is what gives the decorative chrome on a motorcycle its mirrorlike finish.

**An aluminum ingot**

## Precious No More

Aluminum, that humble source of soda cans and foil wrap, was once so difficult to extract from ore that samples were treated like precious metal. At the Paris Exposition of 1855, bars of aluminum were displayed next to the French Crown Jewels. When a pyramid-shaped capstone of aluminum was placed atop the Washington Monument in 1884, the metal was as expensive as silver.

Archaeologists recently unearthed bronze weapons from China's third century BCE that showed no sign of corrosion—because they were coated with chromium. It is primarily mined in South Africa, Kazakhstan, India, Russia, and Turkey.

## Cobalt

Cobalt is a hard, brittle metal, similar in appearance to nickel and iron. This oxidation-resistant metal is valuable for electroplating and in the tool and dye industry. Cobalt forms high-strength alloys, such as those used in jet turbine engines. Cobalt salts produce vivid blue pigments, which, for centuries, have been used in painting, porcelain, glass, pottery, and enameling. Major deposits occur in Zaire, Morocco, and Canada. It is obtained from the ores of nickel, copper, silver, lead, and iron.

Cobalt blue watercolor paint. Although cobalt is a plain silver-gray metal in its ore state, its salts are used to create rich blue pigments.

## Copper

First used by prehistoric humans as far back as 8000 BCE, copper was easy to mine and to smelt (process). Known for its distinctive pinkish gold color (and its blue-green patina), it was called *cuprum* in Roman times, from the island of Cyprus, where it was mined. Today, copper is used in jewelry and the decorative arts as well as in electronics (for wire, circuit boards, relays, switches, and vacuum and cathode-ray tubes), architecture, shipbuilding, plumbing, cookware, and coinage. When copper is alloyed, or combined, with zinc or tin, the result is brass or bronze, two invaluable metals in their own right.

## Iron

The sixth-most abundant element in the universe, iron makes up 35 percent of the earth's mass. Pure iron

**Iron nails**

is extracted from the iron ore hematite, but since it oxidizes rapidly, it is often alloyed with carbon and silicon to create rust-resistant steel. This workhorse metal accounts for 95 percent of worldwide metal production and is made into cast iron, wrought iron, carbon steel, alloy steels, and iron oxides. It is used in building, transportation, science, space technology, medicine, blacksmithing, and hundreds of other applications. Scientists theorize that the first iron used by humans was from meteorites, and the first mining and smelting took place around 2000 BCE.

These days, the Statue of Liberty's color is the distinctive blue-green of weathered copper. The inset shows a model of Lady Liberty under construction and still her original coppery orange.

## ROCK STARS
### Lady Liberty

THE STATUE OF LIBERTY, which welcomes visitors to New York Harbor, is made of copper. Originally a gift from the people of France in 1886, the 151-foot-tall (46 m) statue has weathered over time to a soft blue-green, called patina.

# The Core of Industry continued

## Lead

Lead is a soft, easily worked metal of a dull gray color. It is most commonly extracted from the mineral galena. Although lead use dates back to 6400 BCE, many of its applications have not changed over time: it is still used for building, roofing, plumbing, shot or bullets, weights and fishing sinkers, and as solder. In the Middle Ages, alchemists, or scientists who tried to create gold from less valuable metals, searched for a formula that would turn lead to gold—without success. Lead is poisonous, and exposure to lead paint and pipes should be limited.

## Manganese

Manganese ore is gray, but in other forms this mineral is known for its rich color. Since the Stone Age, humans have used manganese to create pigments. In fact, cave paintings dating from 30,000 to 24,000 years ago contain manganese pigments.

Manganese is a hard, brittle mineral that is often pinkish gray. Pure manganese is chemically active and will burn in oxygen, as well as rust in water. It is widely used in the steel industry as a component of low-cost stainless steel and aluminum alloys. As a dietary mineral, it is present in grains, spinach, soybeans, and eggs. Deposits of manganese ore are common in lakes and bogs. It is mined in South Africa, Ukraine, Australia, India, China, Gabon, and Brazil.

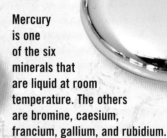

Mercury is one of the six minerals that are liquid at room temperature. The others are bromine, caesium, francium, gallium, and rubidium.

## Mercury

Also called quicksilver, mercury is one of six elements that is a liquid at room temperature. The ancient Egyptian and early Chinese cultures knew of mercury, which they believed prolonged life, even though it is poisonous if consumed.

Mercury is used in thermometers, barometers, sphygmomanometers (a machine that measures blood pressure), and other scientific measuring devices. Although it is one of the rarest metals, and many mines have been depleted, mercury can be extracted from cinnabar and other minerals.

## Nickel

Nickel is a silvery white metal that can be polished to a high sheen; its use dates back to 3500 BCE. It is found in most meteorites and helps scientists distinguish them from other rocks. Nickel resists oxidation, is a fair conductor of electricity, and is used in making stainless steel. Copper-nickel alloy tubing is utilized in desalinization plants that convert seawater into fresh water. Deposits are found in New Caledonia, Australia, Cuba, Indonesia, and elsewhere.

Uranium ore

## Tin

Tin—a silvery, malleable mineral—is called a "poor metal" due to its low melting and boiling point. Tin and copper composed the first alloy, bronze, commonly used by primitive humans around 3000 BCE. The widest use of corrosion-resistant tin is as a coating for metal food containers. Tin is obtained from the compound cassiterite and from various sulfides. It is mined in China, Peru, Malaysia, Indonesia, and Brazil.

## Titanium

Silvery white titanium is lightweight, strong, corrosion resistant, and durable, and has a high melting point. This "space age" mineral is invaluable in the manufacture of planes, ships, submarines, and armor plating. Since the 1940s, the aeronautics industry, the military, and, more recently, the National Aeronautics and Space Administration (NASA) use it when designing rockets and space shuttles. Titanium's biological compatibility also makes it ideal for use in human prosthetics, or artificial body parts. Although there is more titanium in the earth's crust than nickel or zinc, deposits are small and widespread. Russia accounts for nearly one-third of the titanium mined in the world.

A bar made from titanium crystals. Titanium has a high strength-to-weight ratio, which makes it an ideal metal for the space industry, where every ounce may add to the fuel requirements of a spacecraft.

## Uranium

This radioactive element occurs in tiny amounts in soil, rock, and groundwater. Nearly twice as dense as lead, it is the heaviest natural element, with an atomic number of 92. In Naples, Italy, uranium has been found in yellow glass dating back to the first century CE. Uranium is important as a nuclear fuel and in the creation of plutonium. Its various ores are found in Canada, Australia, Kazakhstan, Niger, Russia, and Namibia.

## Zinc

Zinc, combined with copper, was part of another early alloy—brass. Today zinc is used as a coating on iron to prevent rust (galvanized iron), in dry-cell batteries, paints, and in the chemical industries. Zinc, which is found in igneous formations along with lead and copper ore, is mined in Australia, Canada, and the United States.

Zinc has many industrial uses, but it is also an important dietary mineral. If your diet doesn't include enough zinc, you may become susceptible to infections. Zinc deficiency can also cause growth retardation.

# Nonmetallic Minerals

**N**onmetallic minerals either contain no metal or are not used for the metal that they do contain. Their main applications are as insulation, fillers, and filters, and in the welding, chemical, and ceramics industries. This group includes the most common minerals on the planet.

## Apatite

Apatite is the name for a group of phosphate minerals. Apatite, which appears in many forms and colors, got its name from the Greek word meaning "to deceive" due to its similarity to other minerals such as beryl, olivine, and peridot. It appears in all three types of rock, though usually as small fragments. Apatite is also the mineral component of the tooth enamel and bones of all vertebrates. It is valuable as a fertilizer. In the United States, it is used on tobacco plantations to fertilize crops.

A pair of apatite crystals. This mineral is only rarely used in making jewelry.

## Asbestos

Asbestos is the name given to several minerals of different origins with a similar fibrous appearance, including crocidolite, a variety of amphibole, and chrysotile, a form of serpentine. Because asbestos is able to withstand great heat, twentieth-century builders used it for insulation and fireproofing in houses and commercial structures. But asbestos is toxic if inhaled—it can cause cancer and other ailments of the lungs—so much effort has been made to safely remove it from public spaces.

Often spelled "baryite" outside of the Unites States, the word *barite* comes from the Greek word for "heavy."

## Barite

Silvery, metallic barite can occur as a transparent or translucent mineral. It is typically found in lead-zinc veins in limestone and near hot springs. Barite is used chiefly as a weighting agent for fluids when drilling for petroleum, in heavy cement, and in medical applications. Although barite contains the heavy metal barium, which can explode on contact with air, it is safe to handle. It is predominantly mined in the United States, England, South Africa, and Germany.

## Borax

Originally mined from volcanic deposits, most borax now comes from brine or dried-up lakes. It is used for creating glass and ceramics, in putty, cosmetics, and detergents, and in the biochemical industry. Deposits are located in the United States, Turkey, Chile, Tibet, and Romania.

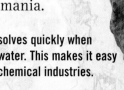

Borax dissolves quickly when added to water. This makes it easy to use in chemical industries.

### Calcite

This abundant, widely distributed mineral displays thousands of crystal variations, and is present in all three types of rock. Varieties of calcite include spar, travertine, chalk, alabaster, onyx, and tufa. Calcite is also the primary mineral in the stalactites and stalagmites found in caves. Large deposits occur the United States, Germany, England, India, Iceland, and many parts of Africa. Aragonite is a harder variety of calcite that forms undersea in coral reefs.

### Dolomite

Pinkish dolomite can appear in large deposits or as veins running through other sediments. Although its crystal form is similar to calcite, dolomite is slightly harder and denser. It is also considered a rock-forming mineral.

### Fluorite

Fluorite occurs in many beautiful shades, from purple and blue to pink, yellow, and green. Fluorite (from which the phenomenon gets its name) also "fluoresces" under ultraviolet light in a variety of hues. It is also used to create iridescent glass, which displays a rainbow of colors as you move it, and as lenses in high-power telescopes and cameras. Deposits are found in Germany, Austria, Switzerland,

England, Norway, Mexico, Kenya, the United States, and Canada.

### Graphite

This soft gray mineral, a form of carbon, is found in both igneous and metamorphic rocks.

It appears as flakes, fine particles, or lumps. A large solid deposit was found in the sixteenth century near Cumbria, England, and was used for marking sheep. Graphite's chief applications today are as industrial lubricants, in brake linings, and as the "lead" in pencils. The main producers are China, India, and Brazil.

People have used graphite to write for centuries. Even its name means "to write" in Greek.

Fluorite is both beautiful and functional. Used to make lenses and other optical (eye-related) elements in very powerful telescopes, the special properties of fluorite allow astronomers to see very distant objects more clearly than they could with regular glass.

The gypsum dunes at White Sands—so soft and cool that children can sled down them—roll like waves in the sea. Wind blows the dunes higher and steeper until they are so steep that they collapse forward, and the process begins again.

## Gypsum

Colorless or white gypsum forms in sedimentary rock when seawater evaporates. Mineral gypsum appears as flattened crystals, as silky fibers, or as compacted, granular masses. The mineral is used for making plaster of paris, sheetrock, and fertilizer. Large gypsum beds can be found in many U.S. states and in Canada, and it is also commercially mined in Pakistan, Jamaica, Thailand, Spain, Italy, England, and Germany.

## Halite

Halite, or sodium chloride, is better known as rock salt. It is another evaporate mineral occurring in dry seabeds. In addition to melting ice on roads and sidewalks, halite is used to make ice cream and as nonlethal shotgun pellets. Large deposits are found in the United States and Canada, and—in the form of salt domes—in Germany, Spain, the Netherlands, and Iran.

## ROCK STARS
### White Sands National Monument

WHITE SANDS NATIONAL MONUMENT in New Mexico features a 25-square-mile (65 square km) deposit of gypsum sand. President Herbert Hoover declared the rolling gypsum dunes a national monument in 1933. Similar dunes appear at the northern pole of Mars.

Milky quartz gets its name from it soft, white, cloudy color. It is one of the least transparent quartz varieties and may, in fact, appear wholly opaque.

### Quartz

Quartz, the second-most common mineral in the planet's crust (after feldspar), is found in all three types of rock. It can be transparent or translucent and appears in a variety of colors. Crystalline quartz includes rose quartz, blue quartz, citrine, amethyst, smoky quartz, and milky quartz. Cryptocrystalline quartz is usually opaque and includes the earth-toned agates, flints, chalcedonies, chert, and jaspers. Opal is a noncrystalline form of quartz.

### Sulfur

This pale yellow, brittle mineral was known since ancient times—the Bible refers to it as "brimstone." After it is mined, sulfur is converted to sulfuric acid, which is then used to make fertilizers, batteries, gunpowder, insecticides, and in other industrial products. Sulfur is found near hot springs and where there is volcanic activity. It is mined in Indonesia, Japan, Chile, and Sicily.

### Talc

The ancient Egyptians and Chinese made use of soft, gray-green talc. Talc is formed when natural forces, usually heat or water, alter magnesium-rich rocks. It can be found in deposits in metamorphic rocks and may be massive, fibrous, or soft. Soapstone, which contains large amounts of talc, has the typical greasy, soapy talc feel. Talc is used in cosmetics, as paint filler, in insecticides, as a lubricant, and as a baby powder to soothe diaper rash.

The smell of sulfur as it burns or as it mixes with air is famously awful, similar to the odor of rotten eggs. It is not, however, harmful.

# Rock-Forming Minerals

![mine cart icon] **A**lthough they have little value as raw materials, the rock-forming minerals play an important role in the creation of the earth's landscape. They also provide the minerals in soil and the salt in the ocean. Nearly all of them are part of the silicate group, meaning part of their chemical makeup is oxygen combined with silicon. Rock-forming minerals are so widespread on the planet's crust that nearly every rock contains at least one of them, yet there are barely a dozen in total.

Scientists label rock-forming minerals "mafic" or "felsic," depending on their compositions. Some rock-forming minerals have both mafic and felsic forms.

**Hornblende can be found in basalt, granite, and many other rocks.**

## Amphibole (mafic)

Amphiboles often display long, needlelike crystals and form wedge-shaped cleavage fragments. Hornblende, a green or black glassy mineral, is the most common member of the amphiboles family and is often seen in igneous rocks.

## Chlorite (felsic/mafic)

Chlorite forms in cavities in igneous rock. It can appear as masses, crusts, fibers, or in bladed crystals. Although the crystals split into thin sheets, they are not flexible.

## What are Mafic and Felsic?

SCIENTISTS COINED THE TERMS *mafic* and *felsic* to describe the components in silicate minerals and igneous rocks. The *m-a* in the word *mafic* comes from periodic symbol for the element magnesium, the *f* comes from iron's periodic symbol, and the *s-i-c* stands for "silicates." These rocks are richer in heavier metals, usually dark in color, and have a specific gravity above 3.0. Basalt and gabbro are typical mafic rocks. The term *felsic* applies to silicate minerals and igneous rocks that contain less heavy metal and more silicates. The *f-e-l* comes from "feldspar" (the potassium-rich variety) and the *s-i-c* from "silicates." Felsic rocks are often lighter in color and have a specific gravity below 3.0. Granite is the most common of the felsic rocks.

## Epidote (mafic)

These complex silicates form in most metamorphic rocks and can be found as pistachio green, brown, or black crystals in seams or as greenish crusts.

**The color of epidote varies with the amount of iron in it.**

## Feldspar (mafic/felsic)

Roughly 60 percent of the earth's crust is composed of feldspar, which is the most abundant group of minerals. Feldspar is found in most igneous rocks and is used in the ceramics industry to produce

**The word *feldspar* mean "field rock" in German. Feldspar forms in magma.**

glazes, enamels, and binders. Zeolites are chemically related to feldspars; they are called boiling stones because they bubble when heated by a blowpipe.

## Mica (mafic/felsic)

Recognizable by its paper-thin, flexible layers, mica includes the minerals vermiculite, muscovite, biotite, and lepidolite. Under the name "isinglass," it was once used to make the heat-proof windows on old-fashioned stoves. More recently, this heat resistance has made mica an important component in a variety of electronic equipment.

A member of the common mica group, lepidolite yields our primary source of lithium, used extensively in electrical engineering.

## Pyroxenes (mafic)

Pyroxenes are closely related to the amphiboles, but they produce square cleavage fragments. Enstatite, a form of pyroxene, is occasionally found in meteorites.

## Quartz (felsic)

Quartz is the final mineral to form in felsic granite and can be found filling in the spaces between other minerals.

## Serpentine (felsic)

Common serpentine, which is chemically similar to chlorite, can occur in colors from white to deep green and black. It can also be identified by its waxy luster and is suitable for carving and polishing.

The word *serpentine* comes from the Latin for "serpent rock" and refers to its typical greenish color and snakeskin-like appearance.

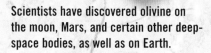

Scientists have discovered olivine on the moon, Mars, and certain other deep-space bodies, as well as on Earth.

## Olivine (mafic)

Olivine is found in magnesium-rich igneous formations, such as basalt. Crystals of the greenish mineral produce a semiprecious gem called peridot.

# Gemstones

Gemstones are the naturally occurring crystalline forms of a mineral. Gemstones are sorted into two categories: precious gems, which are elevated by their beauty, rarity, and hardness; and semiprecious gems, which are more common and less durable.

## Transparent Gems

These gems truly sparkle, capturing and transmitting light with little interference.

### Aquamarine

This pale blue-green beryl is often heated to intensify its color. Sailors once believed that throwing an aquamarine into the sea during a storm would calm the water. Brazil is the leading aquamarine producer, followed by Pakistan, the United States, and China.

Cool blue-green aquamarine is the most common form of the mineral beryl. The application of heat changes the color of aquamarine, even fading it to white.

### Garnet

Garnets form in high temperatures and under extreme pressure, giving them hardness and durability. The relative abundance of deep red garnets has lowered their value, though some varieties, such as the green demantoids and tsavorites, have attained precious gem status.

Peridot is a fairly common semiprecious gemstone, which has even been recovered from meteorites. Although the bright yellow-green of peridot is very different than the deep green of emeralds, some historians suspect that some of the "emeralds" worn by Cleopatra of Egypt were actually peridot.

### Peridot

A gem variety of olivine, peridot, or "evening emerald," has a distinct apple green color. Said to be Egyptian queen Cleopatra's favorite gem, peridot has been mined for 4,000 years. Major deposits are in Afghanistan and Pakistan.

### Tanzanite

This vibrant blue-violet stone is pleochroic (an optical phenomenon caused by the double refraction of light), showing flashes of red-purple and green. Tanzanite was discovered in 1967 in Tanzania—which remains its only source.

## Topaz

Most topaz is colorless or pale yellow when mined, but it also comes in pale and dark pinks, brown, red, and orange. Irradiating, or exposing it to radiation, turns yellow topaz to the popular blue shades. Naturally occurring precious topaz is orange-yellow, while rare imperial topaz is a pinkish orange hue. Topaz is mined in the Ural and Ilmen Mountains, Afghanistan, Sri Lanka, Czech Republic, Germany, Norway, Pakistan, Italy, Sweden, Japan, Brazil, Mexico, and the United States.

Although most topaz is a burnt orange color, it can also occur in shades of yellow, green, pink, and blue.

## Tourmaline

The national gemstone of the Americas, tourmaline occurs in hundreds of shades, including the highly valued copper-bearing popsicle blue Paraiba tourmaline, named for the mine in Brazil where it was found.

## Zircon

Zircon is a naturally occurring gem, unlike cubic zirconia, which is a lab-created diamond. Clear zircons, which produce both luster and fire, have often been mistaken for diamonds. They also occur in greens and browns. Heating them produces striking blues and golds.

# THE FOUR KINGS

THEY ARE THE ROYALTY of the mineral world, and, in fact, the top four gems—diamonds, emeralds, rubies, and sapphires—are known as "the four kings."

### Diamond

Diamonds, which are composed entirely of carbon, are the hardest substance found in nature. Gem-quality diamonds boast high refraction, intense fire, and a range of colors, from the typical white or clear variety to reds, blues, greens—and just about every color of the rainbow. Diamonds formed deep in the earth's mantle before volcanoes located where the crust is thickest carried them to the surface. Most commercial diamonds are mined from kimberlite pipes in the cores of extinct volcanoes. South Africa (and its neighboring countries) is the top source, with mines also found in India, Brazil, Russia, Australia, and Canada. The distribution of diamonds is tightly controlled to keep prices at a premium.

### Emerald

Emeralds, one of the most sought-after gems, are a green variation of the mineral beryl colored by traces of chromium and iron. Even the best emeralds, which are a vivid green with a hint of blue fire, contain inclusions—visible flaws and areas of discoloration. They are mined in Colombia, Zambia, Brazil, Zimbabwe, Madagascar, Pakistan, India, Afghanistan, and Russia.

### Ruby

Rubies are a variety of corundum, a mineral second only to diamonds in hardness. They are renowned for their deep red or "pigeon's blood" color, which comes from traces of the element chromium. Quality rubies are mined in Burma, Thailand, India, Madagascar, Zimbabwe, Sri Lanka, Tanzania, Kenya, and North Carolina.

### Sapphire

Sapphires are also corundum, and, though the majority of stones are blue, they can occur in any color but red. A salmon pink shade called *padparadscha* (Sanskrit for "lotus flower") is highly prized. Deposits are found in eastern Australia, Thailand, Sri Lanka, Madagascar, East Africa, and the United States.

## Quartz Gems

Quartz gems, with their stunning array of varieties, have served throughout history as stand-ins for more expensive gemstones, ranging from clear white diamonds to dense green jades.

## Agate

Agate is the most common form of chalcedony, a cryptocrystalline variety of quartz, and is found in volcanic rock. Typically banded, specimens with straight layers are called riband agate. Stones with layers that form concentric circles are called ring or eye agate. Examples with green filaments that resemble plants are called moss agate. Petrified wood is also a form of agate.

**Banded agate**

## Amethyst

This popular semiprecious gem occurs in a variety of purples, from pale lavender Rose de France to grape-colored stones from Mexico. The color purple has signified royalty throughout history, and amethysts have adorned many kings and queens.

**Amethyst**

## Bloodstone

Also called heliotrope, bloodstone is a deep green stone with red spots of iron oxide that resemble drops of blood.

**Bloodstone**

## Carnelian

This vivid reddish brown stone is a member of the chalcedony family.

Examples of carnelian jewelry have been recovered from Bronze Age ruins in Crete. The stone was also used to make Egyptian scarabs and as a signet ring for sealing messages, since wax did not stick to it.

## Chalcedony

Many opaque gems are part of the chalcedony family. What gemologists refer to as chalcedony is usually the waxy pale blue or white varieties.

**Chalcedony**

## Chrysoprase

This variety of chalcedony is a soft green, colored by traces of nickel oxide. It is mined in Australia, Germany, Poland, Russia, Arizona, California, and Brazil.

**Chrysoprase**

## Citrine

Citrines start out naturally as pale yellow stones, but are often heated to create a deeper orange or reddish tone.

## Jasper

As a gemstone, this member of the chert family traces back to biblical times. It was used as jewelry and carved to make seals and vases. Jasper occurs in shades of red, yellow, brown or green and is often speckled or banded. A variety known as picture jasper shows a miniature landscape, complete with a horizon line.

**Carnelian**

### Onyx

This form of cryptocrystalline quartz can occur in many colors or blends of colors, including green, black, white, tan, and brown. Shaded red specimens containing sard are called sardonyx. When used as a gemstone, onyx is cut and rounded to make rings and beads.

Onyx

### Rock Crystal

Rock crystal is a colorless form of quartz used to create gemstones, prisms, and carvings, such as crystal balls. Mineral inclusions can produce unusual specimens; golden rutiles form hairlike strands in rutilated quartz, while tourmalinated quartz shows a web of black needles.

Tourmalinated quartz

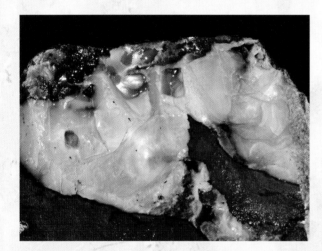

Precious opal shows a rainbowlike iridescence.

### Precious Opal

A silicate gem known for its interior flashes of neon colors (called "play of light"), opal has been mined since Roman times. Today quality opals—including crystal, black, and boulder varieties—come from Australia, Mexico, and the western United States.

### Smoky Quartz

Smoky quartz is one of the few black or brown minerals cut into gemstones. There are several distinct varieties: cairngorm comes from the mountains of Scotland; morion is a deep black, opaque stone; and coon tail features alternating bands of black and gray.

## Gem Cutting

GEM CUTTERS, OR LAPIDARIES, have been cutting and polishing stones since the earliest civilizations began. The four methods used for shaping gems are tumbling, cabbing, faceting, and carving.

Tumbling involves placing stones in a barrel with an abrasive and spinning them until they are smooth. Cabbing—also called cutting *en cabochon*—means shaping a stone with a flat bottom and rounded top. Faceting—or cutting angled planes—brings out a stone's brilliance and fire. Carving involves creating an image on a stone, either by cutting into the stone, called intaglio, or by leaving a raised image above the background, as with a cameo.

Gems can be cut into a wide number of shapes: round, square, oval, trillion, marquis, pear, teardrop, cushion, cross, heart, shield, and baguette. The two most common types of faceting are the brilliant cut, employing triangular- and kite-shaped facets; and the step cut, which arranges rectangular facets on top of each other. Many lapidaries combine both types of faceting. One recent innovation is the fantasy cut, which adds grooves to the facets on the pavilion, or the underside of the stone.

A cut diamond sparkles as the facets catch rays of light.

An uncut stone looks dull compared to its faceted version.

### Opaque Gems

These non-see-through gems come in a wide range of rich colors, from iridescent whites to inky blacks.

**Black hematite with quartz**

### Hematite

This lustrous silver-gray or black stone is often used in jewelry, either to contrast with paler gems or to simulate black pearls. It is mined in England, Mexico, Brazil, Australia, and the Lake Superior region of the United States.

### Jade

Jade is the name given to two separate minerals: jadeite and nephrite (a variety of the mineral actinolite). Archaeologists have found prehistoric jade beads, and ancient peoples used jade to craft weapons. Jade carvings and jewelry made their way from the Far East to Europe along the Silk Road (the trade routes connecting Asia with the Mediterranean world), creating a demand for the cool, waxy stone. Jadeite can be a bright "imperial" green, brown, red, lavender, or many other colors. Nephrite is typically green and white. Jadeite is now mined primarily in Burma and Guatemala, nephrite in Canada.

### Jet

A form of lignite, or brown coal, shiny black jet is fossilized wood. In Victorian England, women often wore jet in mourning jewelry—brooches, necklaces, and rings. Deposits are found in Yorkshire, England; Languedoc, France; Oviedo Province, Spain; and Colorado.

**Lapis lazuli**

### Lapis Lazuli

This deep blue stone with inclusions of pyrite has been mined for six thousand years in the Badakhshan Province of Afghanistan. From ancient Egypt to modern times, lapis has been used for gems, ornamentation, and, when ground up, as a paint pigment called ultramarine. It is also mined in Chile, Russia, Siberia, Angola, Burma, Pakistan, California, Colorado, Canada, and India.

### Malachite

Malachite is a decorative stone featuring swirling bands of green. Malachite often appears in striking combinations with other minerals—deep blue azurite, glittering black mottramite, and baby blue chrysacolla, for example. Deposits are found in Congo, Namibia, Russia, Mexico, Australia, England, and Arizona.

**Malachite with brilliant blue azurite**

Moonstone

### Moonstone/Sunstone

The mineral oligoclase (a feldspar) produces both moonstone—a white gem with glowing opalescence—and sunstone—a gem with red flashes caused by hematite inclusions. The stones are mined in Sri Lanka, New York, Russia, Sweden, and Canada.

Rhodonite with pyrite

### Obsidian

When superheated lava comes into contact with water it forms obsidian, or volcanic glass. Stone Age humans shaped the jagged black or dark brown obsidian stones into cutting tools, and later many peoples of the Americas crafted into weapons or polished it to use as mirrors. Some varieties, such as snowflake obsidian with its lacy white patches, make attractive gemstones.

### Rhodocrosite

This gem's remarkable color—rose pink with a hint of orange—seems to shine from deep within the stone. Unfortunately, the soft, brittle mineral is not practical for everyday jewelry, though clear, large specimens are sometimes faceted for pendants or display.

Rhodocrosite

### Rhodonite

This pink- or rose-colored mineral often contains black veining of manganese or pyrite. A popular gem for carving, it is harder and more durable than rhodocrosite. Rhodonite is mined in the Ural Mountains of Russia, Australia, Sweden, Brazil, Massachusetts, and Franklin, New Jersey.

### Turquoise

Turquoise, which has been mined for more than 6,000 years, might be the most valued of the nontransparent gems. The stones can range from deep blue-green to sky blue, and many specimens show veins of brown matrix. Quality stones come from Iran, Australia, and the southwestern United States, where Native Americans incorporated turquoise into their tribal jewelry and ornaments.

# Earth Gives Up Its Secrets

*M*ining is the term given to the extraction of valuable rocks and minerals from the earth. These raw materials can be found in the form of ore bodies, seams, or veins.

## History of Mining

Mining began in prehistoric times, when early humans first made tools and weapons from materials they found on or near the surface of the planet. Flint was one of the first rocks to be mined. Early humans formed it into spear and arrow tips by a process called knapping, which means that they chipped away at rocks until they achieved the desired shapes. The chalk deposits in Grime's Graves, England, were mined for flint around 3000 BCE. The Lion Cave in Swaziland, South Africa—a source of the hematite used to make ochre pigment for cave paintings—has been carbon-dated back 43,000 years.

## The Rise of Mining

As civilizations rose, the ability to mine intensively increased. The early Egyptians mined malachite, turquoise, and copper to make jewelry and pottery. The Greeks used the profits from the silver mine in Laurium to support the city-state of Athens. The Romans perfected an archaic form of mining gold called hushing, in which they used heat and water to crack open the earth and reveal the precious ore.

In North America, Indians were mining for copper along the shores of Lake Superior 5,000 years ago. The native people of Central and South America also mined gold, silver, turquoise, and precious gems, much of which the invading Spanish conquistadors routed to Europe.

Medieval mines in Europe used the power from water mills to crush ore, bring it up from the pits, and power the bellows that supplied air to the shafts. In 1627, miners in Hungary first used black powder to blast through rocks.

## Modern Mining

Today, mining is big business. International corporations compete for new deposits of iron ore, coal, uranium, precious metals, and gems. These raw materials typically occur in placer deposits—valuable minerals scattered among gravel, sand, or other loose matter, or in lodes—where the target material appears in veins or seams in a mass of rock.

Most modern mining relies on two techniques. Surface mining requires removing layers of soil, plants, and rock to get at the buried deposits. There are several types of surface mining, including quarry,

open-pit, strip, and mountaintop removal. Placer deposits, which are not deeply buried, are most often surface mined.

Subsurface mining involves sinking a shaft into the bedrock and extracting material that is then processed at the surface. Shafts can be excavated horizontally (drift mining), diagonally (slope mining), or vertically (shaft mining).

## Hazards of Mining

Unfortunately, many minerals are nonrenewable resources, meaning that there is a finite supply of them. Once they are gone, they are gone forever.

Overmining at some sites has led to deeper shaft excavations. The deeper shafts create dangers for miners, as well as for homes and buildings above these unstable areas, which become prone to sinkholes. Surface mining scars the landscape and erodes the soil. Both types of mining require chemicals for processing ore, which then contaminate groundwater and soil.

Recently, the governments of many countries have forced mining companies to abide by stricter environmental guidelines with harsher penalties, but there is still a long way to go before mining ceases to be a threat to local ecology.

The El Chino Mine. Chino is an open-pit copper mine located near Silver City, New Mexico. Copper reserves there are expected to last until 2015. Chino is one of the largest open-pit mines in the world, and it is the oldest functioning mine in the American Southwest.

# Meteorites and Moon Rocks

Have you ever looked up into the night sky and seen a shooting star? These bright flashes of light are not stars, but meteors—and if they fall to Earth, they are called meteorites. Meteorites that are recovered after observers see them in the sky are called falls; all others are called finds. Scientists name meteorites after the locations where they are found.

## Meteorites

Mineralogists classify meteorites into several types—86 percent are chondrites, which contain small fused silicate particles and amino acids; 8 percent are achondrites, which are similar to Earth's igneous rocks; and 5 percent are metal meteorites composed of nickel-iron alloys.

An iron meteor from Nandan, China

## Meteor Strikes

During Earth's turbulent history, many large meteorites left gaping craters after striking the planet. Meteor Crater in Arizona (4,000 feet wide/1,220 m) was the first impact crater that scientists verified. Chicuxulub Crater off the Yucatan (110 miles wide/177 km) is the result of a devastating impact that scientists now believe led to the mass extinction of dinosaurs. Vredefort Crater in South Africa (155 to 186 miles wide/249–300 km) is the largest known crater on Earth.

Meteor Crater, near Meteor, Arizona. The gigantic crater is also known as Barringer Crater, in honor of Daniel Barringer. He was the first to suggest that a meteorite impact produced the gigantic hole in the ground.

## ASTRONAUT MATERIAL

A new mineral, armalcolite, was discovered on the moon. It was named for the first three astronauts to travel there: Neil ARMstrong, Buzz ALdrin, and Michael COLlins.

### Moon Rocks

On July 20, 1969, humans first walked on the moon as part of NASA's Apollo program. One important part of the Apollo astronauts' mission was to bring moon rocks back to Earth for evaluation. Altogether, the six Apollo missions collected more than 840 pounds (380 kg) of rocks. But moon rocks already existed on Earth as lunar meteorites—the result of violent cratering events that sent them hurtling toward our planet.

Scientists discovered that most moon rocks were not so different from Earth rocks. They had depleted levels of volatile elements, such as potassium and sodium, but did contain basalt as well as the earth-forming minerals plagioclase feldspar, pyroxene, and olivine. Because the moon has no atmosphere to deflect space debris, small craters also pit the lunar rocks. Scientists estimate that one specimen, called the Genesis Rock, is four to five billion years old, dating from the time the moon solidified.

The Genesis Rock, collected by *Apollo 15* astronauts James Irwin and David Scott, is a sample of original lunar crust from around the time the moon was born.

### A Surprise Discovery

For years, scientists believed that there was no water on the moon. But, in 2008, researchers from Brown University in Rhode Island re-examined rock samples from *Apollo 15* and found minute quantities of water inside ancient volcanic glass bubbles. This raises new questions of how the moon—and the earth—was formed.

### Housing Treasures from Space

The majority of moon rocks are stored at the Johnson Space Center in Houston, Texas, and at Brooks Air Force Base in San Antonio, Texas. The Smithsonian Institution in Washington, D.C., and the Kennedy Space Center, on Merritt Island in Florida, also possess samples. To keep them free of moisture, they are kept in nitrogen-filled cases. Now, 40 years after that first moonwalk, scientists continue to unlock the mysteries of these extraterrestrial rocks.

Next stop, Mars. Images taken from the Mars Pathfinder site of rocks believed to have been strewn about by ancient rivers give NASA mission planners a strong motive to send human geologists to the Red Planet. This artist's rendering depicts two such scientists. NASA hopes to one day send a mission to Mars that would collect samples of Martian rocks, just as the Apollo missions collected lunar rocks.

# Rock Hounds: A Collecting Guide

Natural history museums are great places to start researching rocks and minerals. Many of them have impressive collections from around the world, such as the Museum of Natural History in New York City. A 4.5-ton (4 metric tons) pillar of azurite/malachite ore greets visitors to the Harry Frank Guggenheim Hall of Minerals.

**W**atch out! Collecting rocks can quickly become a full-time hobby. You may start out with a few interesting rocks that you gathered locally, and, before long, you're scanning the Internet for exotic samples or trading specimens with collectors in distant lands.

## Where to Begin

A good first step for the beginner rock hound is to visit a gem shop. Here, you'll find samples, both large and small, of hundreds of rocks and minerals. Talk to the owner and point out which rocks interest you. Do you want to collect geodes or crystals? Or, are you more interested in volcanic oddities? The owner can guide you to inexpensive specimens, help you identify the rocks you've already collected, and tell you about good locations to prospect in your area.

If you hear that there is going to be a gem or rock show nearby, try to attend. You'll learn a lot from the experts and get to see rocks and minerals from all over the world. The rocks and minerals exhibit at a local museum is also a great place to learn the basics of identification.

If you are thinking of starting a collection of your own, visit a gem and mineral shop to check out what kind of rocks and minerals interest you most. Your next step will be finding out where those samples can be found in nature.

### Playing it Safe

Old quarries, riverbanks, and abandoned mines are all good places to search, but they can be dangerous for inexperienced hunters. It's better to start looking on nature trails, along shallow streams, or around—not inside—excavation sites. Never climb dangerous rock faces in search of specimens or take rocks from the bottom of rock piles that might start to slide. Find a "rock buddy" and go hunting with your friend, or ask your science teacher to take your class on a collecting field trip.

### Showing Off

At home, you can display your collection on a bookshelf or wall shelf. Large specimens look great on a coffee table or fireplace mantel. A special lighted stand for crystals shows off the inner beauty of your find. You can identify your specimens with small paper labels on the bottom.

### ROCK HOUND'S KIT BAG

Here are some basic supplies you'll need before you go rock hunting.

- A sharp-ended rock hammer for separating samples from the bedrock
- Leather gloves
- Plastic goggles and face mask (some rock dust can be harmful if inhaled)
- A collecting pouch or backpack
- A magnifying lens to examine crystals or layers in rock faces
- A stiff brush for cleaning dirt from your specimens
- A pocket guidebook for field identification

As you collect more specimens, you might want to invest in a rock tumbler, which turns rough, dull rocks into smooth, colorful stones that you can make into jewelry by using wire wraps or by drilling holes in them with a Dremel tool, which can be found in hardware or art supply stores.

Happy hunting!

Rock hammers come in several sizes, so rock hounds can dig up many kinds of samples. Most large hardware stores sell suitable hammers, although they may not be labeled as rock hammers.

# Find Out More

**WORDS TO KNOW**

**aggregate.** Materials used in construction, including sand, gravel, and crushed stone

**alloy.** A substance composed of two or more metals

**aphanitic.** A fine-grained rock with such a compact texture that the minerals that make it up cannot be detected with the naked eye

**atom.** The smallest component of an element having the chemical properties of the element

**brine.** Water saturated or strongly impregnated with salt; the sea or ocean

**cabochon.** A carved, polished gem stone with a smooth rounded top and flat bottom

**crystal.** A solid body having a characteristic internal structure and enclosed by symmetrically arranged plane surfaces, intersecting at definite and characteristic angles

**eon.** An indefinitely long period of time

**evaporate.** When heat extracts, or takes out, moisture or liquid from something, making it dry or reducing it to a denser state

**felsic.** Rocks consisting chiefly of feldspars, feldspathoids, quartz, and other light-colored minerals

**glacier.** An extended mass of ice formed from snow falling and accumulating over many years. Glaciers move very slowly.

**igneous.** Rocks produced under conditions involving intense heat, such as rocks of volcanic origin or rocks crystallized from molten magma

**ion.** An electrically charged atom or group of atoms formed by the loss or gain of one or more electrons

**isotope.** Any of two or more forms of a chemical element, having the same number of protons in the nucleus, or the same atomic number, but having different numbers of neutrons in the nucleus

**impurities.** Trace minerals that can change the appearance of a mineral

**mafic.** Rocks rich in iron and magnesium

**magnet.** An object, such as a piece of iron or steel, that possesses the property of attracting certain metals, such as iron

**matrix.** The fine-grained portion of a rock in which coarser crystals or rock fragments are embedded

**metamorphic.** Rocks that undergo structural and chemical change due to heat or pressure

**molecule.** The smallest physical unit of an element or compound, consisting of one or more like atoms in an element and two or more different atoms in a compound

**mollusk.** Any invertebrate, or animal without a backbone, or spinal column, typically having a chalky shell of one, two, or more pieces that wholly or partly enclose the soft body

**oxidation.** The combination of a substance with oxygen, which changes the structure of the substance

**patina.** A film or encrustation, usually green or blue-green, produced by oxidation on the surface of bronze, copper, or other metals

**phaneritic.** Coarse-grained rocks in which the main minerals that make

them up are visible to the naked eye

**pharaoh.** The title of an ancient Egyptian king

**obelisk.** A tapering, four-sided shaft of stone, usually having a pyramid-shaped top

**organic.** Characteristic of, pertaining to, or derived from living organisms

**radiation.** The process in which energy is emitted as particles or waves

**sedimentary.** Rocks formed by the deposition of sediment

**symmetry.** The correspondence in size, form, and arrangement of parts on opposite sides of a plane, line, or point

**vertebrate.** An animal possessing a backbone, or spinal column

## BOOKS TO READ

Bailey, Jacqui, and Matthew Lilly. *The Rock Factory: The Story About the Rock Cycle* (Science Works). Mankato, MN: Picture Window Books, 2006.

Blobaum, Cindy, and Michael Kline. *Geology Rocks! 50 Hands-On Activities to Explore the Earth* (Kaleidoscope Kids). Nashville: Williamson Publishing Company, 1999.

Dussling, Jennifer. *Looking at Rocks* (My First Field Guides). New York: Grosset & Dunlap, 2001.

Edwards, Ron, and Lisa Dickie. *Diamonds and Gemstones*. New York: Crabtree Publishing Company, 2004.

Grabham, Sue. *Backpack Books: 1,001 Facts about Rocks and Minerals*. London: DK Publishing, 2002.

Pellant, Chris. *Rocks and Minerals* (DK Eyewitness Books). London: DK Publishing, 2004.

Pinet, Michele, and Alain Korkos. *Be Your Own Rock and Mineral Expert* (For the Junior Rockhound). New York: Sterling, 1997.

Pough, Frederick H., Roger Tory Peterson, and Jeffrey Scovil. *A Field Guide to Rocks and Minerals* (Peterson Field Guides). New York: Houghton Mifflin, 1998.

Prinz, Martin. *Simon & Schuster's Guide to Rocks & Minerals*. New York: Simon & Schuster, 1978.

Ricciuti, Edward. *Rocks and Minerals* (Scholastic Science Readers). New York: Scholastic, 2002.

Schumann, Walter. *Gemstones of the World*. New York: Sterling, 2007.

Shaffer, Paul R., Herbert S. Zim, and Raymond Perlman. *Rocks, Gems and Minerals* (Golden Guide). New York: St. Martin's, 2001.

Squire, Ann O. *Gemstones* (True Books: Earth Science). New York: Children's Press, 2002.

Stewart, Melissa. *Extreme Rocks and Minerals! Q&A*. New York: Collins, 2007.

Symes, R. F. *Crystal and Gem* (DK Eyewitness Books). London: DK Publishing, 2007.

Ward, David. *Fossils* (Smithsonian Handbooks). London: DK Publishing, 2002.

Wilk, Harry. *The Magic of Minerals*. New York: Springer, 1986.

## WEB SITES TO VISIT

John Betts Fine Minerals
www.johnbetts-fineminerals.com

Rocks and Minerals for You
www.rocksandminerals4u.com

Rockhound Kids
www.rockhoundkids.com

Rockhounds
www.fi.edu/fellows/payton/rocks/

Rocks for Kids
www.rocksforkids.com

Rocks, Minerals, and Fossils for Kids
www.rocksmineralsandfossilsforkids.com

## WHAT'S YOUR BIRTHSTONE?

CERTAIN GEMS HAVE LONG BEEN ASSOCIATED with particular months. Since the first century CE, people have given gifts of these "birthstones" as symbols of good luck. The gems vary between different traditions, although the gem's color for a particular month usually stays the same. Ayurvedic birthstones date back to ancient India (1500 BCE); mystical birthstones come from Tibet and date back more than 1,000 years; traditional stones date back to about the 1500s in Europe; and modern birthstones were standardized by the American National Association of Jewelers in 1912.

| Birth Month | Ayurvedic | Mystical | Traditional | Modern |
|---|---|---|---|---|
| JANUARY | Garnet | Emerald | Garnet | Garnet |
| FEBRUARY | Amethyst | Bloodstone | Amethyst | Amethyst |
| MARCH | Bloodstone | Jade | Bloodstone | Aquamarine |
| APRIL | Diamond | Opal | Diamond | Diamond |
| MAY | Agate | Sapphire | Emerald | Emerald |
| JUNE | Pearl | Moonstone | Alexandrite | Pearl |
| JULY | Ruby | Ruby | Ruby | Ruby |
| AUGUST | Sapphire | Diamond | Sardonyx | Peridot |
| SEPTEMBER | Moonstone | Agate | Sapphire | Sapphire |
| OCTOBER | Opal | Jasper | Tourmaline | Opal |
| NOVEMBER | Topaz | Pearl | Citrine | Yellow Topaz |
| DECEMBER | Ruby | Onyx | Turquoise | Blue Topaz |

# Index

# Credits